Making, Not Breaking

The First Year Under Saddle

Making, Not Breaking

The First Year Under Saddle

Cherry Hill

Photographs by Richard Klimesh and Cherry Hill

🐎 **Breakthrough** 🐎
PUBLICATIONS

For information address:
Breakthrough Publications, Inc., Ossining, New York 10562

Printed in Mexico

ISBN: 0-914327-43-7

Library of Congress Catalog Card Number: 92-071026

Acknowledgments

Thank you to the following individuals for help in preparation of this manuscript:
Richard Klimesh
Todd Mowrer

Thank you to the following individuals for being photo models:
Sue Dixon,
Richard Klimesh,
Students in the Colorado State University Training Classes,
and Steve and Mike Bowers of Bowers Brothers Horse Training.

Illustrations by Peggy Judy (unless otherwise noted).

Contents

Preface

When a human and a horse stand facing each other in a training pen, neither one of them *wants* a fight. And neither one of them *wants* to be frightened. They basically want to get along. If the goal is a long-term

partnership, then they must reach an understanding and an effective system of communication. They must watch each other carefully, listen acutely, and respond honestly. The trainer needs to make the rules and be in charge. But, in order for the partnership to be successful, the rules should be based on the natural instincts and talents of the horse.

For a human to win, it is not necessary for a horse to lose. A human should not take things away from a horse or break him into fragments in order to train him; rather the trainer should *add* to the horse. The goal should be making, not breaking, the horse.

Horse training styles have varied according to the changing characteristics of society, the purpose for the training, the type of horses being trained, and other factors. In the United States, the development of the West brought about a style of training referred to as breaking. Out of necessity, horses became accustomed to the world of humans rather abruptly so that they could be used for ranch work after a very short training period. People who totally discredit breaking may not realize that, as with any style of training, among cowboys there were and are good horsemen as well as poor horsemen. A good horseman has respect for horses and works toward a dependable partnership. Poor horsemen treat horses with disrespect, often handling them with excessive force.

In the past, the role of the horse was utilitarian. Today, horses are used primarily for recreation. It is no surprise, then, that modern training methods are characterized by cooperation rather than domination. With the increased technology in all aspects of modern life not only have we experienced an information explosion but an increased awareness and desire for natural living as well. As a result, a number of low stress, "natural" training approaches have recently emerged. However, these methods to a large degree are nothing new; they are based on classic, practical, proven techniques of horse training that have withstood the test of time. The new approaches simply use inviting modern words and phrases.

Over the years, I have learned and tested various training systems before blending them to suit my goals, personality, time schedule, the type of horses I work with, and so on. That is why I advocate a training procedure that is a combination of the best aspects of western and dressage techniques. The eclectic approach I present is suitable for the foundation training of any horse whether destined for English or

Western use. I want my horses to be versatile: to be well schooled in the arena yet safe and sensible in a variety of real-world riding situations. The material in this book is suitable for the initial training of a young horse or for the re-training of an older horse that missed out on the basics. I hope that what I offer you here will help you to develop your own personal training style.

Although it is necessary to establish dominance over a horse, harsh methods and continual confrontation only serve to develop resentment in a young horse. Such an attitude can remain with a horse its entire performance career and continually thwart your efforts. On the other hand, avoiding confrontation at all costs with a soft and permissive approach often results in the horse assuming the role of an undisciplined pet rather than a honest partner. So don't be hard and don't be soft— be firm. Allow confrontations to occur if they happen naturally because they are one way in which a horse learns. But don't make a big deal out of mistakes. Be matter-of-fact and business-like as you iron things out. If you are respectful and fair as you teach your young horse the rules, you will lay the foundation for a successful and long-lasting partnership.

How much knowledge do you need to be a successful horse trainer? Although knowledge rarely hurts anyone, the lack of it almost always does. As with other sports, it helps if you know the rules and strategies ahead of time. Learn all you can about horse psychology and the mechanics of training. But do your intellectualizing before you climb in the saddle so you do not have to think things out while you ride. That way you can concentrate on communicating with the horse's body through your body. An excessively cerebral approach to horse training can complicate things and could make you so mentally preoccupied that you are less effective when it comes right down to sitting on the horse and riding. After all, training horses is a very physical activity.

To be a successful trainer of young horses, you must thoroughly understand horse behavior, know how to read horses, and you must understand the principles involved in training. You need to design your training program to develop a horse, not conquer him; to enhance his potential, not destroy his natural abilities; to encourage him to do simple things well rather than force him to do advanced things poorly. Devise a plan that is organized yet flexible enough to meet each horse's individual and changing needs.

Your goal should be willing obedience and cooperation from the horse. Although a well-trained horse of any type, should, in fact, submit to the dictates of the trainer, submission does not in any way indicate the horse has a broken spirit. Rather, the horse had been encouraged to cooperate with the trainer's wishes because throughout his training the right things have been made easy and comfortable for him to do and the wrong things have been made difficult and uncomfortable. Horses, by nature, are generally cooperative and interested in developing an interaction with humans. So don't make the mistake of viewing a horse as your adversary.

To effectively work with a horse, you must know yourself, know horses, and see a clear distinction between horses and humans. Be careful not to develop anthropomorphic thinking. Anthropomorphism is attributing human characteristics to animals. Horse owners some-times think of their horses as members of the family. While it is understandable that you may develop a great deal of admiration and affection for a particular horse, it is important that you see a distinction between your roles, needs, and behaviors.

For one thing, horses don't think about a situation like you do, they simply respond to it. They don't reason and take into consideration your intentions, they just react to what is happening. For example, although you may be able to convince yourself that a penicillin injection is for your benefit, a horse only reacts to the injection itself. If a horse has had incompetently administered injections in the past, you can't talk the horse into relaxing by saying you are trying to help him, you simply must very capably administer the injection.

The same goes for training. Although you may be trying to teach a horse something "for his own good," if you don't know how to effectively show him what you want him to do, you will end up frustrating him . . . and yourself. If you want him to learn how to move away from your leg so that he carries himself in a straighter, more balanced fashion (which is much better for his muscle development in the long run and better for him mentally because he won't have to repeatedly receive the heel of your boot), you must know how to position him correctly and ask him to respond using the language of reflexes and behavior modification.

This book will provide you with that kind of information as well as some food for thought to chew on in between rides. I've written this as a thinking person's training book rather than a cookbook. Besides telling you *what* you need to do, I've tried to explain *why* you do it and *how* you do it. That way when things don't go "according to the book," you will be able to figure out what to do!

I have written this book as a sequel to *The Formative Years, Raising and Training the Young Horse from Birth to Two Years,* which left off just as you were ready to put your foot in the stirrup for the first ride. No matter how old the horse is that you are currently working with, be sure he has received thorough ground training as outlined in *The Formative Years* and the more advanced ground training covered here in *Making, Not Breaking.*

For continuity and interest, I have used photographs of three of the horses that were models in *The Formative Years:* the suckling/weanling; the yearling; and the dark two-year-old. I wanted you to see the progress of those horses several years later in the hands of novice and experienced trainers. I have also included some photographs of students in one of the colt training classes at Colorado State University. The riding and training experience of the students ranged from novice to quite experienced. I asked some of the students to demonstrate proper and improper training methods for my photographs and I appreciate that they were willing to do that for me.

One thing that a trainer at any level of experience needs to constantly improve is the quality of his or her riding. *If you are not a balanced, correct rider, you can not hope to achieve optimum success with an untrained horse.* Never be too proud or stubborn to seek or accept professional help with your riding and training. United States Olympic riders and most top U.S. competitors receive regular coaching and training, so why shouldn't you?

Although it is important that you learn to recognize when a problem stems from a horse's blatant misbehavior, don't automatically blame a young horse for a problem. First take a good look at the effectiveness of your riding skills. I have not covered riding per se in *Making, Not Breaking* because I have already written a book which addresses that topic specifically. It is called *Becoming an Effective Rider* and I encourage you to read it so that you can hone your riding skills and offer your young horse the very best chance for success.

I hope that you have a good horse under you and that you take your time and enjoy the experience—after all, isn't that the reason we all got into horses in the first place?

July, 1992   Cherry Hill

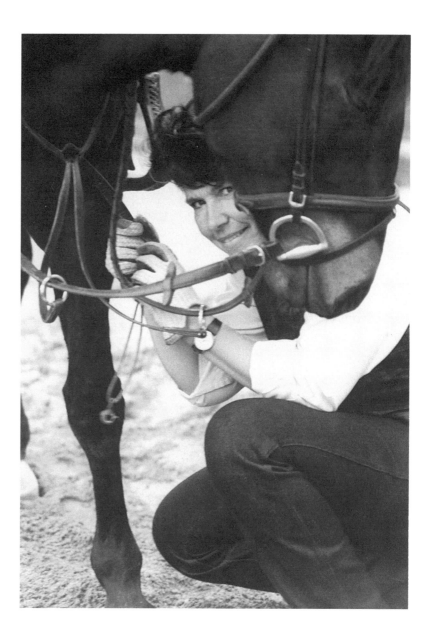

1

Training Philosophies

Training Defined

*3. (below left)
When asked to yield
to the rider's right
leg and bend to the
right, this horse
reacts by raising his
head and stiffening
his back.*

*4. (below right)
Through proper
application and
release of the aids,
he learns to bend
cooperatively around
the rider's inside leg
in a soft and
compliant arc to the
right.*

Training has many valid definitions. In psychological or behavioral terms, training replaces a horse's inborn fear of man's world with respect, trust, and a willingness to learn. In physiological terms, training contains a horse's energy. First, the energy seems to flow somewhat randomly in a relatively large vessel that has somewhat flexible boundaries. Little by little the horse's energy is condensed and organized so that it fits comfortably in a smaller container with somewhat tighter, more clearly defined boundaries. One of the goals as the horse's energy is being channeled into a workable shape is to keep the energy calm. If the energy becomes too excited, it may spring a leak, damaging the boundaries of the smaller container you have been carefully creating.

Training provides the incentive for a horse to change his habits from what *he* may want to do to what *you* want him to do. There is a saying among horse trainers that we basically ask horses to do the opposite of what they want to do. We ask a slow horse to hurry up; a fast horse to slow down; we make a horse that likes to bend to the left, bend to the right; we want a horse that holds his head very high to lower it; we want a horse that hangs his head low to elevate it. The art of training is knowing how to provide aids and incentive that encourage the horse to work correctly (photos 3 and 4).

Training is characterized by dynamic relaxation. Dynamic refers to something happening, characterized by motion and energy. So how does relaxation fit in? When a horse knows what is expected of him and is physically capable of complying, he has the capacity to relax his mind and body as he works. This does not in any way infer the horse moves lazily with a slack or inattentive attitude. Rather it means that the work proceeds with calm energy, with a certain controlled intensity and alertness that is necessary in order for learning to take place. Be sure that you do not confuse relaxation with inattentiveness or laziness.

Training makes the right things pleasant and easy and the wrong things unpleasant and difficult. By understanding the principles and procedures involved in training a horse, you can set your horse up for success by making the right responses easy for him. Some trainers feel that you should never let a horse know that the wrong options exist, especially when referring to dangerous behavior like bucking and rearing. Yes, certainly, if you can avoid it, you should never let your young horse realize he can buck while you are riding him. It can develop into a long-standing habit. But this thinking, that of preventing mistakes, should not be taken too literally. After all, having mistakes tactfully corrected is a powerful way to learn in many instances.

Training involves separating the means from the goals. Where you are going is not as important as how you get there. The means used to develop a young horse are far more important than attaining a certain goal at a certain time. Of course, having goals is a healthy way to approach a training project, but goals should be viewed as of secondary importance to the quality of the daily work.

Training requires an honest evaluation of a horse's strong points and weak points. The successful trainer builds on a horse's strengths rather than attacking his weaknesses. Such trainers base their work on their own strong points as well. That way, both the horse and trainer can improve, gradually strengthening their weak areas. It is important that you preserve your horse's self-esteem as well as your own during the sessions. That way you will both look forward to the work with a positive attitude.

Training involves compromises. It might seem ideal for a horse training project to go "textbook perfect" but that simply doesn't happen. All along the way, you will experience variations in results. You will have to assess and modify your plan. Such observation and alteration will eventually become second nature. You need to be willing to leave some things alone while you are working on others; you cannot work on it all at once. In the early training as you teach the lope or canter, in order to maintain forward motion and balance, you may need to allow your horse to lope more energetically than the ideal. You must compromise your expectations related to the energy level of the lope because of the more important, early goals related to forward motion, relaxation, and rhythm. Later, as your horse develops, he will be able to lope slowly *and* retain his balance. But if you are impatient about the speed or length of stride of the lope and make an issue out of it, you may destroy his desire to go forward and carry himself in balance. Making wise compromises is part of the art of horse training.

Training requires conditioning. It involves the development of a horse's body for the work he is to do. It includes the strengthening of the muscles, heart and lungs, legs and hooves, and the mind. You cannot tire out a horse completely with longeing before you ride and still expect things to go well. A horse must have the mental and physical strength to do things correctly. A tired horse will more likely do things wrong because he cannot muster physical energy or concentrate mentally. Once a young horse has a base of conditioning, you can begin challenging him more both physically and mentally. Trying to teach an exhausted youngster his lessons, however, is not only unfair but it usually is counterproductive.

Behavior

Successful training is dependant on a thorough knowledge of horse behavior. Often horses' actions are interpreted as wanton misbehavior, when in actuality they are instinctual reactions. While a horse's inherent behavior needs to be altered in order for him to be ridden, basing the modifications on already existing instincts and reflexes results in minimal stress and long-lasting results.

Whether or not there is action, there is behavior. A sullen horse, rigid and unyielding, is behaving just as much as the wildly bucking one. And any behavior that is repeated becomes habit, even though it was not formally designed as a lesson. Horses are constantly learning as a result of their handling and the environment.

Even though the modern horse is relatively safe from predators, its historically long struggle for survival has resulted in a deeply imbedded suspicion of anything unfamiliar. Because of this, the modern horse is one of the few domestic animals that still retains the instincts necessary to revert to a wild state. These instincts make the horse awe-inspiring and frustrating at the same time.

The horse is a gregarious nomad with keen senses, deeply ingrained instincts, and highly developed reflexes. These characteristics are what send a horse to the winner's circle as well as sending a panic-stricken horse through a wire fence. If you understand the nature of the horse, you can use it to your advantage.

Gregarious animals are sociable within a herd and tend to live and move in groups. Given the choice, horses are rarely seen alone. They prefer to be in close proximity to other members of their species. Safety and comfort are found in numbers. An entire band panicking from an illusive beast, a group huddling against the wind or snow, and preferred associates participating in social rituals are natural, gregarious behaviors.

Horses typically perform daily routines in response to various needs. At particular times of the day, herds can be observed to eat, drink, roll, play, and perform mutual grooming. The desire to participate in these rituals is not diminished, and in fact is often intensified, for the horse in confinement. In spite of bathing, clipping, and blanketing, most horses love a good roll in the mud, much to the chagrin of the groom! The old adage, "You can lead a horse to water, but you can't make him drink" is based on firmly implanted habits that are governed by a biological clock. Many routines are socially oriented—small groups grazing in tight-knit bands on huge ranges, a contagious pawing and rolling session, playful running and bucking.

Just because horses desperately want to be with other members of the band, however, doesn't mean all horses get along well. Especially when there is limited food or space, personality conflicts will surface. Battles may be fought with teeth and hooves or merely a threatening gesture. Once the clash is over, a pecking order or dominance hierarchy emerges. This social rank makes future aggression unnecessary unless a particular horse is not thoroughly convinced of his status and continually tests the horse immediately above him. The most assertive horse generally earns his choice of feed, water, and personal spaces.

Humans occupy a rung on the ladder of power as well and are tested by various horses to see just where they stand. You must convince each horse you work with that you are on a higher rung. One way to establish this is at feeding time. But do not make a big deal of this; just do what you have to do matter-of-factly and go on. As you approach a feeder, a horse may come forward aggressively, perhaps with his ears back and a bullish body language. He is telling you in the language he would use with another horse to get away from his feed. The worst thing you could do at that point is to reward the horse for his aggressive behavior by dumping the feed and leaving. Instead, make the horse back off until you give a clear verbal signal such as "OK," that the horse may now approach the feeder.

Sometimes a horse may innocently attempt to interact with you as if you were a horse. While a young horse is being groomed, the sensation often causes him to want to reciprocate by nibbling as he would to a herd mate during mutual grooming. Even though the gesture is intended to be friendly, it must be discouraged or you may one day find that the horse will use his teeth to give you an unforgettable back rub.

If a horse has not been sufficiently socialized with humans to the point that he feels secure away from other horses, he may desperately attempt to retain communication with or proximity to a preferred associate. The classic case is often referred to as barn-sourness because the insecure horse links comfort, companionship, and food with the barn. What may have originated in an immature horse as a temporary insecurity may evolve into a long-standing and dangerous habit.

The horse is a born wanderer. This nomadic tendency is responsible for precipitating confinement behaviors such as pawing, weaving, and pacing. These vices are a response to inactivity, lack of exercise, over-feeding, and insufficient handling. Regular exercise is necessary for the horse's physical and mental well-being. Adequate turn out space and play time prevent the development of neuroses.

Horses that are kept in box stalls or small pens need to be turned out and allowed to "be horses." Otherwise they may become either very bored with their existence or extremely hyperactive. A chronically bored individual who has tuned out may be lazy, unresponsive, and irritable. The hyperactive horse is anticipatory, nervous, and unsafe.

Keen senses allow the horse to pick up slight changes in the environment (photo 5). Often more sensitive to subtle movements, far-off

5. This horse detects subtle changes in the environment that are disregarded by his human handler.

sounds or vibrations, and smells than you are, horses are frequently alerted to potential danger while you may notice nothing out of the ordinary.

When the horse is convinced that danger is imminent, he almost always chooses to flee rather than to fight. It is the rare horse that on his own volition will stick around and assess the situation in the event he might be imagining things. Horses can be taught to trust the judgment of their trainers, however. The trail horse left to his own devices would probably avoid the "black hole" that in reality is only a 8-inch-deep creek. When a trainer (who treats her mount fairly) asks the horse to give it another try, the trusting but skeptical animal will reconsider. As long as the trainer makes wise decisions and never asks the horse to negotiate something unsafe, the horse's natural instinct of fear can be overridden by his faith in his trainer.

If, however, a horse lacks confidence or has received poor handling he can behave very irresponsibly and will spook with the slightest provocation. Because a horse has an excellent memory, he will remember quite remote experiences especially if they relate to his real or imagined safety. It is thought a horse can never quite forget such fears. All you can hope for is to encapsulate the bad experiences with layers upon layers of good ones.

Suppose a horse is out on a road ride and is passing a familiar farm. The horse is relaxed and unsuspecting. All of a sudden, a bleating billy goat runs out of the yard, hopping on three legs, the other tangled in a tether rope which has bobbing on its other end a child's brightly colored plastic "tractor-bike." The horse's senses of smell, sight, and hearing are understandably put on red alert and his subsequent intensity of behavior will depend on his temperament and training. Even if the horse agrees to stand still while the situation calms down, he will be innately suspicious of that farm on each succeeding ride. In order to allay the horse's apprehension, you must systematically plan good experiences at that spot. Make arrangements with the owner of the goat to have it contained so that the horse can approach. Let the horse have a rest break there. Feed the horse on location if necessary. Convince the horse that more good things than bad occur at that particular spot.

Much of training is designed to modify or systematically override a horse's natural reflexes. (See the discussion on reflexes in Chapter 2.) For example, it is an automatic, protective response for a young horse to raise his leg when it is touched. Although this is beneficial when teaching the horse to pick up his hooves for cleaning, there are times (such as when bandaging or clipping) when you will want to handle the horse's legs without them moving. You will need to use a combination of reflex training principles and desensitization to help a horse learn what you want him to do. The roots of a horse's behavior constitute the basis for our attraction and fascination with him. By understanding behavior and developing sound training principles, you will have a greater chance of success.

When to Start

When should you start your young horse under saddle? Answers range from eighteen months to five years. I prefer to start my own horses in the fall of their two-year-old year. I will ride them at least a half dozen times and maybe up to thirty or forty times, depending on the individual. Then they are turned out on pasture for the winter to continue developing mentally and physically. In the spring of the three-year-old year, once they have shed, they are put in a moderate but regular training program until late fall. They are turned out once again for the winter. Then from the spring of their four-year-old year on, they are kept in active work year round.

Trainers who start horses in the fall of their yearling year usually do so in order to exhibit them in futurities and/or to be able to sell them as quickly as possible to get a return on time and money investment. Such business motives often put unhealthy pressures on a young horse both mentally and/or physically. Some can take such stress, others cannot.

Some who start riding yearlings say that a trainer is able to shape a yearling's mind and body before he has developed set patterns of behavior or movement. That benefit must be weighed against the increased probability of problems such as splints, stress-related injuries, and various types of mental and attitude problems.

At the other end of the spectrum are trainers who wait many years to start a horse under saddle. Sometimes this is for good reason because of an injury or late development. In many cases of late mounting, however, it is found that the horses are quite resistant to changing their habits. If a horse is a slow developer and won't be ridden until he is four years old, it is important to keep the horse on a regular training program, even if it just involves in-hand work, longeing or driving, and developing good barn manners.

When you start a young horse is not as important as *how* you start him and *what* you work on. Set your priorities in a reasonable manner and work on things in order. Plan the work, then work the plan. (Chapters 5 and 6 cover the process of training in detail.) For example, do not start working on headset with a young horse. That is about the most backward way to start the training of the horse, yet it is a surprisingly common approach. Instead of focusing on the head, develop a natural, comfortable movement from the hindquarters, and the head will take care of itself. Introduce new elements based on the results you are receiving, not on the amount of time you have spent at a particular stage. Watch your horse's progress, not the clock or the calendar.

Take plenty of time to make the basics very clear to your young horse. The basics are the lessons covered in the first few months of a horse's training and are the foundation of any horse's intermediate and advanced work. When an advanced horse has problems with a complex maneuver his trainer can go back and work on basic principles that the horse solidly learned in his two-, three-, and four-year-old years. If a horse does not have a foundation, you will have nowhere to go to begin a review. You will have to start all over from the beginning. So take the time to clearly establish the early lessons. It will save you a great amount of time and frustration in the long run.

Although my training philosophies and principles are designed to be universally applicable to many horses and events, each trainer, horse, and situation will be slightly different. I encourage you to read all of the information offered and then devise your own individual training plan for the horse with which you are currently working.

Stages of Training

Even though there will be some variation among the methods and progression of a horse's lessons depending on his eventual use, most initial training has the same goals. The horse must be safe to handle from the ground and safe to mount and ride in a variety of circumstances. The horse needs to be obedient to the aids, supple and relaxed, relatively straight in his travel, and appropriately balanced in his movements. These are the basic guidelines for the early training of any horse, from a dressage horse to a classic western horse.

FAMILIARIZATION PHASE

During the early lessons the young horse must become accustomed to the training routines and sensations. This includes the feeling of a saddle on his back, cinch restriction, the bit in his mouth, a person on his back, sweating without being able to rub, following a work routine, and so on (as I have shown in photo 6). In addition, the horse will be introduced

6. During the familiarization phase, the horse must become accustomed to tack and the training routine.

to the mental concentration that will be required of him so that he can pay attention for progressively longer periods of time. A horse should be relaxed and relatively comfortable about all of this.

QUANTITATIVE PHASE: OBEDIENCE TO THE AIDS

Willing and correct responses to the rider's aids must be cultivated early in the young horse. During the quantitative phase, you have many objective training goals. First your horse must be taught to move forward in response to the signal from the pressure of your legs on his ribs. The simplest form of this lesson is halt to walk.

Your horse must then learn to accept regulation of his forward movement by paying attention to your seat and the action of your hands through the reins to the bit. When you still your seat and close your hands on the reins and no longer apply leg aids for forward movement, your horse should decrease or cease forward movement. The simplest form of this lesson is the walk to halt transition.

Gradually your horse will begin to accept the connection you make from leg aids to rein aids and will be asked to perform other transitions and maneuvers. This is the process of getting a horse "on the bit" or "in the bridle." Some of the more basic transitions are: walk to trot; trot to walk; trot to canter; canter to trot.

Your young horse must also learn to move his hindquarters away from your leg when it is applied actively on his side behind the girth. This is termed leg-yielding and is the precursor to all of the lateral movements.

During the technical skills phase of a horse's training, he learns what to do and what not to do. He learns a battery of responses which his trainer desires. He amasses his repertoire of basic skills: walk, trot, canter, turn left, turn right, stop, bend the body, yield to the trainer's leg, back up, stand still, and so on.

QUALITATIVE PHASE: IMPROVING FORM

In the qualitative phase, the horse learns how to perform his newly learned skills in a smoother, more balanced manner. In other words, he improves the quality of his work. The horse first learned *what* to do, now he learns *how* to do it in better form. Of course, the quantitative

7. This young horse is stepping forward into light contact with the bridle as the rider's lower legs squeeze him on the ribs.

phase and the qualitative phase are not separate phases. All along you will be shifting back and forth between teaching a horse what to do and then helping him learn how to hone his performance. Throughout the horse's qualitative training, there are certain subjective goals to keep in mind: forward energy, rhythm, suppleness and relaxation, mental and physical acceptance of contact, relative straightness, balance, and precision.

Forward Energy

Your young horse should learn to step forward when your lower legs squeeze his ribs (illustrated in photo 7). As he progresses in his lessons he develops a self-motivated forward driving force from his hindquarters that not only propels him ahead but also supports his (and your) weight as he moves. This is the very beginning stage of the more advanced goal of self-carriage. Self-carriage is a manner in which the horse moves forward energetically on his own volition, without being propelled by the rider and without being dependant on the rider's aids to hold him in a balanced form.

Rhythm

A horse knows his gaits inherently and performs them in a rhythm dependant on his conformation and development. In early mounted lessons a horse learns *when* to perform each gait. Then he learns to perform each gait in a steady, regular rhythm. When a horse quickens his pace, stumbles, or has an irregular rhythm, it is an indication that he has lost his balance. To help a young horse develop a solid rhythm, you need to follow his movement without interfering with his balance.

Once a regular rhythm is firmly established, you will have an easier time altering the rhythm if necessary. If you are aware of the timing and direction of movement of each of the horse's legs, you can influence his movement with aids that ask the horse to emphasize a particular component of his movement rather than confusing him by asking him to move against his existing momentum. For example, if you are in tune with the rhythm of the horse's hind legs at various gaits, you can sit deeper at the proper moment and slow your horse down. Or you can apply leg aids to energize a particular hind leg as it pushes off. Getting in sync with a horse's rhythm is a prime example of your responsibility to be an effective rider *before* you attempt to train a horse.

Suppleness and Relaxation

All throughout a horse's training, from the first ride to the most advanced, he must be mentally and physically relaxed in order to perform at his best (see photo 8). It is essential that the horse accepts the

8. This three-year-old is moving forward well and is relaxed and ready to be put on the bit and go to work.

bit, that he is not afraid to move forward into the bit, and that he is responsive to signals from it. This takes a fair amount of time to accomplish. You can encourage the horse to relax by sitting balanced and offering a steady contact on the reins and allowing him to stretch into his natural rhythm. The more consistent you are with your aids, the more relaxed the horse will become.

A relaxed, supple, young horse would be characterized by a low frame, a content expression, a swinging back, a tail that swishes back and forth with the movement of his hindquarters, a soft working of the bit in his mouth, often with the production of saliva, and either periodic or regular blowing or snorting.

Mental and Physical Acceptance of Contact

Early on, the horse learns that the rider's driving aids make him go forward and the restraining aids make him stop. Eventually he will need to learn that both the driving aids and restraining aids will be applied simultaneously, encouraging him to rebalance his body rearward. Contact, accomplished properly, occurs when the driving aids cause the hind legs to step up under the horse's supple back and the resulting energy meets the soft but steady restraining influence of the rider's hands on the horse's mouth. Attainment of contact should never be attempted by pulling backward. A horse must accept connection with the rider's entire body without physical tension or mental resistance.

Relative Straightness

The early lessons teach the horse to walk relatively straight from point A to point B, along an arena fence or down a road. Eventually he will learn how to move more technically straight whether he is going around a corner or down the middle of the arena (photo 9). His hind legs will need to follow in the tracks of his front legs, rather than make another set of tracks offset to one side or the other. Most horses have one side with more stretchable muscles and one side with more resistant muscles. The more stretchable side is often weak; the resistant side is less flexible and often very strong. This difference in flexibility of a horse's sides can cause him to travel hollow, stiff, or crooked. Appropriate conditioning work and lateral exercises will help a horse develop so that he can travel straight.

9. One goal is to be able to ride in a straight line. This rider is doing a good job with a two-year-old.

Balance

Balance refers to equality between the left and right sides as well as equilibrium between the forehand and hindquarters. The degree of left-to-right balance a horse displays depends on the level of straightness in his work. To carry more weight on his hindquarters, the young horse must learn to counteract the natural tendency of his weight to fall on his forehand. The more he is able to carry his weight on his hindquarters, the closer he will be to being collected. Collection makes the horse lighter in the rider's hands and will allow the horse to change gait and direction smoothly, without loss of form or impulsion. You should hint at the concept of collection in the later stages of training the young horse, but concentrated work on collection should not begin until the horse has had at least four to twelve months of physical development training.

Precision
First a young horse learns to lope, then he learns to lope on the correct lead from a trot. As he progresses, he learns to lope from a walk, he learns to lope at a precise location, and he departs in balance. The precision of his responses take years to hone.

2

Training Principles

Behavior Modification

Through *behavior modification*, you influence and develop your horse's natural behaviors and reactions into a useful format. There are four ways to modify a horse's behavior: positive reinforcement, negative reinforcement, punishment, and extinction. When a horse acts according to your desires, and you want to encourage him to repeat such behavior in the future, you need to reinforce that behavior. When his behavior is undesirable, you need to indicate that to him by discouraging the behavior, then showing him a different way to act, and then rewarding him when he exhibits the new behavior.

Whether you use positive or negative reinforcers, they should be immediate, consistent, appropriate, and brief. A good trainer is an objective observer, only noting *actual* behaviors, not *interpreting* a horse's actions.

POSITIVE REINFORCEMENT

Rewarding a horse for good behavior by giving him something pleasant following the desirable behavior is reward or *positive reinforcement*. This encourages the horse to repeat the behavior in the future. Although not always handy for routine training situations, giving a horse a food treat is interpreted by the horse as a reward. But horses can also be conditioned to appreciate other actions as rewards. A word of praise or a soothing pat on the neck can also tell a horse he has done something correctly. (Photo 10 shows the horse receiving a conditioned reward.) These kinds of positive reinforcers are often more convenient for everyday horse training. (For further information, see the following section on application of positive and negative reinforcers.)

The demands of training often require intense concentration and physical exertion on the part of a young horse. That is why it is important to periodically reward him during lessons to keep his mental attitude fresh and enable his body to respond properly. A reward not only tells a horse he is doing well, it builds his confidence, and it adds to his enjoyment of the work. It is not feasible for you to elaborately reward a horse after each properly performed movement, yet there are ways to assure a horse that he is working well.

Many riders fall into one of two categories when it comes to doling

10. A horse can be conditioned to interpret a pat as a reward for work well done.

out rewards. Some who are quick to use punishment to correct a horse take the same horse's good behavior for granted and are sparse with rewards. This may be caused in part by a reluctance to "not make a move" when the horse is working correctly or it may be due to a philosophy that the horse should continue along unless the trainer tells him to do things differently.

Other riders may attempt to use rewards to soothe or bribe a horse into good behavior or may lavish rewards on a horse with such intensity and frequency that the reward no longer has a productive effect on the horse. The horse cannot sort out exactly what behavior is being reinforced and what behavior to continue. Some horses can come to expect and even demand reward for just about any behavior. So, to be most effective, a trainer must understand how reinforcement works and find a middle ground.

Since negative reinforcement is so closely related to positive reinforcement (they both encourage a behavior), it is helpful to discuss negative reinforcement before general reinforcement rules. The behavior discouragers, punishment and extinction, will be discussed later.

NEGATIVE REINFORCEMENT

Removing a negative stimulus once a horse has performed a desired behavior is termed *negative reinforcement.* When teaching a young horse to move over while tied, you must teach him to move away from pressure on his ribs. Using a finger or other object, the trainer taps the horse in the ribs until he takes a step sideways, and his reward is that the tapping on the ribs ceases (as demonstrated in photo 11). Each time it will take less negative stimulus to get the horse to move sideways. Soon just a light finger tip will guide him. He has been trained by negative reinforcement. This lesson will carry over to the first time the rider asks for the horse to yield to the leg. Pressure is applied with the heel of the boot until the horse moves away from the leg, then the stimulus ceases.

11. Moving a horse over by using the butt end of a whip is a form of negative reinforcement. When the horse moves, the pressure from the whip handle is removed.

Application of Positive and Negative Reinforcers

Positive and negative reinforcement are both designed to encourage a particular behavior in the future. Together they can be thought of as reinforcers—actions by a trainer to encourage desirable behavior.

Things that a horse inherently perceives as either positive or negative are *primary* reinforcers. Examples of positive primary reinforcers are food, a scratch on the withers, a rest break; negative primary reinforcers are pressure on the mouth and a spur on the ribs. The horse does not have to be taught to feel good about positive primary reinforcers or bad about negative primary reinforcers—his reaction to them is intrinsic.

Secondary reinforcers must be learned. Positive secondary reinforcers are much more common in horse training than negative secondary reinforcers. Although a gruff warning could be thought of as a negative secondary reinforcer because the horse has learned that this sound means he had better not do something wrong, a verbal scolding after the fact would technically be classified as punishment which will be discussed later.

Positive secondary reinforcers are things which the horse learns to appreciate such as a pat or a kind word. To teach a horse to perceive a secondary reinforcer as a reward it should be initially linked with a positive primary reinforcer. For a horse to respond to the trainer's voice as a reward, consistent words, tone, and inflection must be used at times when the horse is receiving a primary reinforcer. For example, if you were to say "Good Boy!" in a pleasant, praising voice as you fed your horse a treat or as you released the reins so he could stretch his neck, when you later used the phrase during a training situation, it would tend to elicit a sense of contentment in the horse and he would likely relax and stretch.

In order for a secondary reinforcer to retain its conditioned effect, you must periodically refresh the horse's memory by linking primary pleasurable experiences with it. Using a variety of primary reinforcers (rest, scratching, feed) will make a stronger, more long-lasting connection. Using a secondary reinforcer too many times ("Good Boy" at every step), or without periodic substantiation, may result in it losing its effect. The overused reinforcer may no longer represent contentment to a horse; it can lose its importance to the horse.

It takes a trainer with good knowledge, a keen sense of feel, and good reactions to reward a horse properly and effectively. The young or inexperienced horse must be rewarded even though his awkward attempts are far from the ideal. The experienced rider will recognize the successive approximations to the eventual desired behavior and will assure the horse throughout training that he is on the right track, so to speak. A rider who has experience only with advanced horses might find it difficult to recognize and subsequently reward a young horse's attempts.

In order for reward to bring optimum results, the reward must occur immediately after the behavior it is reinforcing, it must appear consistently each time the behavior does (at least at first), it must be of the proper intensity and duration, and it must be a reward appropriate to the type of work and the temperament of the individual horse.

Food is a very appropriate reward to teach a horse to come and be caught or to stand still when turned loose. During ground work such as longeing and long reining, however, if food were used as a reward, it may encourage the young horse to come into the center of the circle toward the trainer. During riding training, food rewards aren't really practical either. You would have to adjust the reins to one hand, search your pocket for a treat, bend over to offer it to the horse—it simply is too awkward and comes too late. Giving the horse a treat after dismounting would reward the horse for standing still, perhaps, or for lowering his head and shaking it at the end of the work but not for the previous nice lope depart or the good steps of leg-yielding. Treats that are given at nonspecific times can show a horse that you are generally pleased with him and they may improve his interest in you; but treats more often than not teach a horse to be pushy, to nibble, and to be disrespectful of your space.

During a riding session, there are several effective ways to show a horse he is doing well. Many horses respond positively to a hand on the withers. This stems from the innate social behavior of mutual grooming in which two horses demonstrate their bonding by massaging each other along the spine. Simply letting your hand rest on the withers or giving a few soothing strokes relaxes and softens most horses into lowering the neck and reaching forward.

I have seen some riders deliver a loud slap to the horse's shoulder or on the ribs just behind the saddle when a horse has done particularly well. To me, it hardly seems like something which a horse would naturally enjoy, yet I have observed horses that appear to tolerate it or have learned to associate it with the rest break which usually accompanies the slap. One way to determine what type of touch reward your horse inherently prefers is to turn him loose in a stall or small pen and try a stroke on the neck, a scratch with the fingers on the withers, a slap on the neck, and a flat clap on the flank. He will clearly show you which he intrinsically interprets as reward.

Another way to reward during a training session is to let the horse rest and fill up on air after he has worked hard. This does not mean "throwing the horse away" (removing all aids abruptly so the horse falls on his forehand), but allowing him to walk on light contact or stand quietly for a minute. Rest and stretching into a long or loose rein also reinforces the work immediately preceding and should be interspersed in the lessons, especially those requiring a tendency toward collection.

The release of pressure, or yielding to the horse, when he is performing properly is the reinforcement cornerstone in dressage work and classical western training and should be regularly implemented in the training of any horse. *Yielding means a softening of the active aid, not a giving away of what has been gained.* Normally, a certain degree of yielding should occur at each instance of compliance. If done correctly, this would result in such frequent softening that there would be little chance that you will become stiff or try to hold your horse in position.

The more you learn to yield each time a horse makes a positive action, the more you will encourage the horse to develop a sense of self-carriage. He will develop the notion of using his body in balance based on his own motivation without being dependant on your aids to hold him together. It is somewhat of an honor system—you give the horse a little slack, so to speak, and see what he does with it. Does he fall on his forehand terribly or fling his head up or let his shoulder bulge out, or does he hold himself together a soft and balanced frame as if there were invisible forces guiding him? A young horse will only be able to show you self-carriage for a few steps or so at a time. This is something that you will gradually develop in the young horse.

Sometimes the restraining forces of the back, seat, legs, and hands must be used to an explicit degree in order to keep a horse from "running through" or ignoring the aids. But once the horse complies, there must be a yielding. If you prod a horse constantly with the spurs, hold him rigidly with the hands, and drive forcefully with the seat without letup, the horse has no means, no incentive to learn compliance. The rider who does not reinforce a horse's good movement with a softening teaches the horse to become very tough or to look for an explosive way to evade the relentless aids.

PUNISHMENT

When you administer something unpleasant to a horse to discourage a certain behavior, you are *punishing* him. Sometimes all that is necessary is a verbal reprimand, but often physical discipline is needed to make a lasting impression on a horse. If a horse refuses to stop when you are leading him, you may have to resort to a chain over his nose so that when he tries to run over you, you can apply pressure on the chain to discourage that from reoccurring. As the horse is disciplined with the chain, a voice command ("WHOA") should be used simultaneously, so that eventually the voice command alone will produce the same results. Physical punishment is automatically administered to a horse by an electric fence. When a horse misbehaves by leaning over a fence, he is shocked and subsequently discouraged from repeating that behavior.

Always use the least amount of force or punishment necessary to get the job done. Starting out at a low intensity leaves you room to increase the intensity as needed and assures that the horse is being treated fairly and humanely. However, it is also important to be assertive enough to successfully complete the job. Continual nagging by ineffectively bumping the horse's side with every stride or repeatedly tugging on the bit may not only serve to develop resentment in a horse but may desensitize him to the use of future low-level stimuli.

Punishment must be administered immediately or a different behavior might be punished. A subjective rule of thumb is that for punishment to be effective, the reprimand must be delivered within one to two seconds after the undesirable behavior. If a horse bites you while you are in the process of turning him loose and you are caught off guard and the horse ends up getting loose, the horse has rewarded himself for a bad behavior. Your inclination may be to catch the horse and punish him but then you would be punishing him too late and you would teach him to not be caught in the future because he was punished for being caught. Therefore, what you must do is catch the horse, reward him for being caught, and then as you prepare to turn him loose again, set the stage for him to repeat the bad behavior of biting so that you can punish him. But be prepared to hold onto him. Pretend turning him loose several times until you feel he has given up the biting attempts, then turn him loose.

EXTINCTION

Extinction is the removal of something pleasant to discourage the behavior it follows. Unfortunately, a horse that whinnies noisily at feeding time gets a reward for his obnoxious behavior every time he gets fed. To extinguish the noise, you should not feed the horse when he is noisy, but instead wait until he is quiet, and then give him his feed. With extinction, however, the animal's undesirable behavior usually becomes greatly amplified and embellished before it diminishes — things get worse before they get better. The horse will whinny louder and louder and may add stamping, snorting, and pawing. Understandably, this is the time when many people give in, but it is precisely at that time when the behavior is about to disappear. After a few rewards for being silent, the horse will begin to associate quiet behavior with feeding time.

If a horse has learned that when he speeds up and gets strong in the bridle, his inexperienced rider will take her legs off his sides and loosen the reins, the horse has learned that he can get something good (release of leg and rein pressure) by speeding up. When a capable trainer confronts the horse about this habit, the trainer is using extinction to change the horse's behavior. The trainer no longer allows the horse to have the pleasant outcome of release, and instead holds the aids on the horse. As expected, things will get worse before they get better. The horse will try frantically to push through the aids because in the past he was successful at achieving the pleasant state of not having to comply with the rider's aids. But this time, the capable trainer wins and as soon as the horse finally submits by softening and slowing down, the trainer yields with the aids. Once the horse has initially submitted, it will take less and less time for the horse to soften. Soon the horse will be retrained by extinction and will automatically have a soft and relaxed movement upon application of the aids.

SHAPING

Once a horse has a pretty strong notion of what he should or should not do as a response to a particular set of aids, you should begin to ask for gradual improvement in form. This is called *shaping* or *reinforcing* successive approximations to a desired behavior.

When first teaching a three-year-old a canter depart, you might settle for any type of depart as long as it doesn't include bucking or running away. You begin to hone the transition until the horse not only canters on the correct lead from a trot or a walk but does so with proper balance, rhythm, and engagement. Getting to that stage involves a series of steps that spans many lessons. The horse must be rewarded each time he gets closer to the eventual goal.

Principles to remember as you shape your horse's behavior are:

* Pick the best base to begin with. In the preceding example, it would make sense to the horse if the first time you asked for canter, you were riding in a familiar longeing pen and you used a voice command which you had previously used in longeing or long reining; or if someone in the center of the circle gave that command or signal. It could be dangerous and less productive to take the horse into a large field and kick strongly with both legs. It is best to start on a solid, familiar base.

* Reward all approximations to the desired behavior. If a horse bolts into a canter, you should not punish and can even praise the horse for his attempt. Be especially careful not to bump the horse's mouth as this would be interpreted by him as punishment for cantering. Even if a young horse takes the wrong lead, it is often a good idea to reward him for at least cantering before you try again for a particular lead. Soon the horse will relax, respond to your positioning aids and the correct response will come easily.

* Do not go too fast toward the goal. If you try to reach perfection in just a few lessons, the horse may be missing valuable connections between the maneuver's components. If you expect a balanced, collected canter too early, you may lose forward motion and cause your horse to get behind the bit. The beauty of following a systematic training scheme is that when you have problems, you always have a progression that can be reviewed.

* Do not get stuck in one particular stage. If you are three-quarters of the way to the ultimate goal but you no longer gear the lessons for forward progress, it will likely be more difficult to move the horse on to a more advanced behavior. If during the latter stages of initial training, the horse is allowed 6 or 7 trot strides in between a transition from walk to canter, it may be more difficult to suddenly eliminate them all than to systematically decrease their number. Keeping the lessons moving in a progressive fashion will yield maximum performance and satisfaction.

Closing comments on learning. Although training books, by design, must be written in somewhat of a step-by-step format, horses do not always learn things in a linear fashion. That is, once you get past the first few rides you may find that there is no longer a strict order to the lessons. Also, at various times, you will recognize the need to ride on a plateau for a period, repeating and reinforcing exercises before bringing in something new. There will also be times when you will emphasize a previous lesson. In contrast to some aspects of ground training (in-hand, tying, restraint), there are very few things involved with riding which need to be dealt with by a confrontation. In other words, you rarely should need to bring something to issue when mounted. The majority of the time, it is best to work for gradual progress rather than an all or none reaction. Use patience and planning to bend your horse rather than break him.

Reading a Horse

In order to predict a horse's behavior, you must know how to read horse expressions and body language.

Expression is largely a reflection of temperament and attitude. While temperament is the general consistency with which a horse behaves, attitude is often a temporary reaction to current conditions. Although management and training are usually responsible for a horse's attitude, a horse's temperament is predetermined and relatively fixed. If you find you are working with a horse that consistently has an undesirable or dangerous temperament, I urge you to consider replacing that horse with one that has a disposition more suitable for training.

A horse with a good temperament is alert but calm, he pays attention but is not excitable or explosive. He is sensible, not self-destructive or bull-headed. He is accepting, not testy. When he is faced with something new, he may challenge the limits initially but once he finds that he is being controlled by tack or trainer, he accepts the control and does not repeatedly test his limits. This shows that he has a strong power of association and a high degree of trainability.

The most desirable horses are moderately sociable with humans, that is, they have a healthy respect for humans and enjoy interactions with them. Sociability is partly what promotes a willing attitude. A willing horse has an interest in his work and voluntarily tries various responses to the aids in an attempt to find which response the trainer is after.

Part of a trainer's job, then, is to constantly evaluate a horse's behavior and determine what caused the behavior. To that end, a trainer must be an astute, objective observer. Become proficient at reading the details of facial expression, body posture, and actions to predict what behaviors they precede.

Angry: Ears pinned, head extended, tail clamped.

Bored: Not looking up or out, ears flaccid, head down.

Distracted: Looking around, moving hindquarters from side to side, maybe pawing, not responding to the aids or overreacting to them.

Excited: Swerving, swinging, pawing, calling, defecating, sweating, overreacting to the aids.

Dull: Long reaction time with a low intensity reaction.

Alert: Listening, ears tuned to trainer.

Belligerent/testy: Large, bold movements, head high, muscles
   pumped up.

Sore: Short, timid steps or very stiff movement, often with ears
   back.

Tired: Uncoordinated, stumbling, inattentive to aids.

Silly: Shaking head, sashaying back and forth, tail up high.

Afraid: Either showing characteristics of excitable horse or frozen
   without any reaction to stimuli.

Relaxed: Head low, back slightly arched and swinging, tail held
   off anus and swaying with movement, contented snorting or
   blowing through nose.

It is helpful to learn to read each individual horse. Pay attention to
signs of exertion so that you know when the horse is working hard. Is
he grunting? Holding his ears at half mast? You need to recognize when
a horse is making an effort and when you can ask him for more. You
need to know when you have gone past a horse's point of mental
concentration or past the level of his physical condition. Pay close
attention to the rhythm of his breathing, the movement of his ears, and
the carriage of his tail.

When a horse does something other than what you have asked, you
need to be able to determine if he is, in effect, saying to you:

1. I am confused. I don't know what to do. OR
2. I am tired. My body is not ready to do this. OR
3. Do I have to? Can't I do this instead? OR
4. No. I don't have to obey you.

Some horses are selective listeners. They only respond to what they
want to "hear." For example, you take a fresh horse out to free longe.
He has been longed many times before. He immediately breaks into a
fast trot and you say "walk" and make sure your whip is low and that
your motions are smooth as you move toward his head. There is no
response from the horse—he just keeps trotting quickly. He acts as if he
has never heard or seen this request before. So you decide to move the
horse up to a lope for ten minutes. Then you ask him again for a walk,
and lo and behold, he instantly melts into the ground at a soft walk. His
"hearing" sure improved!

Reflexes

Reflexes are automatic responses to pressure on or movement of various portions of the body. The intensity of the reaction will vary depending on the horse's physical makeup (thin skin, fine hair coat, hot- or cold-blooded, etc.), temperament, experience, training, physical restriction, degree of relaxation or tension, and how forcefully and with what the pressure is applied. Each horse will react differently to various levels of pressure. A horse that is tired, willful, or resentful can override his reflexes by tuning out your aids as a means of protection or defense. Some reflexes are interrelated or are part of a chain of reactions. Figure 1 illustrates the reflex zones that are described in this box.

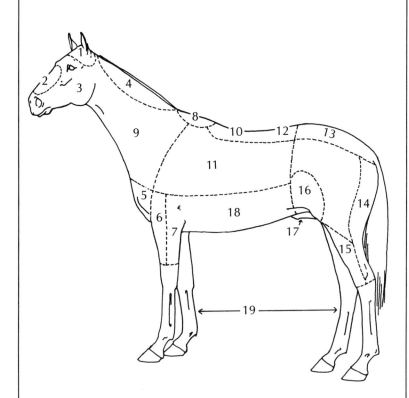

Figure 1. Reflex zones.

1. **Poll.** Pressure here causes a horse to raise his head and neck and perhaps try to pull away.

2. **Bridge of nose.** Pressure here initially causes a horse to raise his head, hollow his neck, and flip up his nose. Systematic use of a chain lead or a bosal can condition the opposite response.

3. **Head.** With no alteration in a normal neck position, an upward head extension causes forelimb flexion and hind limb extension. When the horse's head is down, this causes hind leg flexion and foreleg extension. The parotid salivary gland is a large, long gland stretching from the base of the ear to the throat. When the head and neck posture is up and flexed, the gland is stimulated to produce saliva.

4. **Crest.** Touching here causes a horse to lower his neck.

5. **Breast.** If the horse's head is low, pressure here causes the horse to back up. If the horse's head is high, the reflex tends to be blocked.

6. **Forelimb extensors.** Pressure on the muscles at the front of the foreleg causes the cannon and hoof to swing forward.

7. **Forelimb flexors.** Pressure on the muscles at the back of the foreleg causes the knee to bend.

8. **Withers.** Light pressure causes the horse to lower his head, reach with his neck and nibble if he is scratched. Heavy pressure causes him to evade the pain, possibly with threatening gestures with his head and neck.

9. **Neck.** The neck contracts on the side it is touched. With no alteration in normal head position, hollowing of the neck to one side induces hind leg flexion and foreleg extension on that side; a rounding of the neck results in foreleg flexion and hind leg extension on that side.

10. **Back.** (the spina prominens chain) Light pressure on spine from the withers to the lumbosacral junction will cause the horse to hollow his back. Light pressure on one side, the left for example, will cause the spine to curve away from the pressure and move the left hind leg forward.

11. **Ribs.** When the horse's head is turned toward you, pressure on the ribs causes him to flex his ribs away

from the pressure; his hind leg on the same side also flexes while the opposite hind extends causing sway or crossing.

12. **Loin.** Pressure causes the back to flatten or round.

13. **Croup.** Pressure causes the horse to tuck his tail and hindquarters and round his back.

14. **Semitendinosus.** Pressure causes the horse to raise his leg and/or kick backward.

15. **Gaskin.** Pressure causes hock flexion.

16. **Flank.** Pressure causes the horse to reach his hind leg forward or cow kick.

17. **Sheath.** Pressure may cause the horse to flex both hind legs and drop the croup.

18. **Abdominals.** Depending on the horse's back reaction, pressure on the abdominals can result in a contraction of the horse's belly, a rounding of the back, a lowering of the croup, an arching of the neck, and perhaps a lowering and reaching forward with the neck.

19. **Lower limbs.** Pressure causes upward withdrawal by flexion of joints.

20. **Cutaneous trunci or panniculus.** The sheet of muscle under the skin of major mass of the body reacts to light stroking with rapid repeated twitching; firm, steady pressure causes tonic contraction.

The most successful horse trainers realize that horses do not think things out ahead of time and plan their behavior. Horses act according to inherited instincts and precepts of behavior and react to a trainer's movements and touch with a deeply ingrained set of reflexes. A reflex is an automatic, unconscious response of a muscle (or a gland) to a stimulus.

Natural selection favored horses who escaped their predators because of highly developed instincts and reflexes. Horses are capable of quickly assuming thundering speeds from a standstill, of rising and running instantly from a lateral recumbent sleeping position, and of striking or kicking in the blink of an eye. These lightning-quick reflexes also allow today's horse to perform in a vast array of athletic events.

There is a very important distinction between horses that are trained to respond to a rider's *aids* and those that are trained to respond to *cues.* Aids are based on physical reflexes; cues are dependant on the horse's memory. An example of an aid is that when a rider applies the right leg behind the girth, it causes the horse's hindquarters to move to the left. This aid can be used in combination with various applications of other aids to develop many different individual maneuvers. A cue, on the other hand, is a single signal for the horse to perform a particular maneuver. For example, simply moving the right leg behind the girth might be the signal for the horse to canter on the left lead.

Aids are based on a horse's reflex responses and so, initially, the horse's reactions may be sudden and somewhat rough. Eventually, through desensitization and repetition, reflex responses can be tempered to an optimum intensity so that the horse's body can be made to move correctly and with quality of movement as well.

Cues rely on the horse remembering a past association and a learned response. Therefore, cues can be the cause for anticipation. They are sometimes referred to as "buttons," magic signals that a rider can use to tell a horse what to do. Because of this, cues are often the means used to get a horse to do tricks. Because the horse either responds correctly to the cue or does not respond correctly, the rider has less ability to affect the quality of the various parts of the response.

Because reflexes are unconscious reactions, they can be a potential danger. A horse does not think before responding; he responds automatically. Fortunately, it is possible to override reflexes by training a horse to respond in more acceptable ways. In some cases, your goal will be to completely override a horse's reflexes; in other instances, you will want to modify his reflexes; and in certain situations, you will want to sharpen a horse's reflexes.

The reflexes of the relaxed horse may be slightly slower to respond to your aids than those of an excited horse, but a relaxed horse is also less likely to explode. Be aware of accidental cues or conflicting signals you may give a horse. For example, as you clean out his hooves: Is your hair or your hat tickling his abdominal muscles and setting off reflex contractions? Is the horse covered with reflex-triggering flies?

USING REFLEXES WHEN RIDING

When riding, you must coordinate *all* of your aids so that no contradictory signals are given and so that you elicit the desired composite reflex
actions. When you apply a single leg on the horse's side in the middle
position ("at the girth") it will cause the horse to flex his hind leg forward
on the same side. Applying that same leg behind the middle position
will cause the horse to move his hindquarters away from your leg. Using
both legs in the middle position will cause both hind legs to flex and
subsequently cause the horse to move forward.

Use of the back and upper body via the seat bones can cause one of
two reflex actions or a reaction somewhere in between. Pushing
strongly on both seat bones will likely cause a young or poorly muscled
horse to hollow its back. Pushing moderately and following will cause
the horse to drop his croup, engage the hindquarters, and go forward
with a slightly arched spine. The rider's use of both lower legs on the
ribs causes abdominal contraction which will complement the latter
desirable back reflex.

Weighting one side of the body via the seat bone usually causes the
horse to arc the spine around that seat bone. In other words, if you rock
onto your left seat bone, it causes your horse to bend his neck to the left
as well as causing his hindquarters to curl slightly to the left. If your left
leg is moved well behind the cinch, however, it could cause your horse
to hold his hindquarters straight or move them to the right.

A sideways pull on a corner of the horse's mouth causes the horse to
bend his neck to that side. A pressure against a side of the mouth
generally causes the horse to raise his head and push against the
pressure. A backward steady pull of both reins initially causes a horse
to respond by quickening his pace and raising his head.

Knowing the Aids

Learning to feel and to develop the use of your aids is essential before
you try to train a horse. Remember, you need to develop yourself thoroughly as a rider before you can hope to be a successful trainer. The
more physically fit and supple you are, the better job you will do training
and developing a young horse.

Understanding the composite effects of aids is more important than memorizing "sets of aids" or "cues" to get a horse to perform various maneuvers. Learn how to ride by approaching it as a series of coordinated body movements rather than memorizing what buttons to push. For example, instead of thinking, "canter to trot," think "shoulders back, sit deep, squeeze with both hands while driving with the lower legs" and you will likely find that your horse has made the transition from a canter to a trot. This way you feel how your various body movements create various reactions in your horse. And you can more accurately focus on which of your aids are working and which need development.

You influence a horse through the use of your natural aids and the employment of some artificial aids when necessary. Your natural aids are your mind, seat, upper body (weight), legs, hands, and voice. Artificial aids are pieces of equipment that accent or augment your natural aids. Such items as spurs, whips, and martingales are considered artificial aids. Your aids and influences should not be applied in a haphazard manner.

* Aids should be fair and not contradictory. They should be applied humanely and so that a horse can understand them in equine terms. Aids should not be conflicting or it would be impossible for a horse to respond properly to one aid without being punished by another.
* Aids should be appropriate. You could train a horse to stop when you blew a whistle but would that be convenient or appropriate? Following classic riding guidelines is the best bet.
* Aids should be clear and direct. A horses does not reason, so you must make your signals to him in a direct line of communication, not something he must figure out. Know the level of training of the horse so that your aids will be delivered appropriately for him.
* Aids should be consistent. Each time you want the horse to perform a particular maneuver, you should ask him in the same way he has been asked in the past.

* Aids should be precise and applied at the right moment so that you make it easy for your horse to do the right thing. Your sense of timing will improve with practice, so it is best not to attempt a very complex maneuver until you have the ability to coordinate all of the aids.

* Aids should be applied in the appropriate location. You must know horse reflexes and how a horse will react to stimuli applied in various regions of his body. If you are trying to get a horse to move his right shoulder to the left, it would make no sense to use your right leg behind the girth as this might actually tend to make him turn on his center which would move his shoulder to the right. Similarly, if you are carrying a whip in your left hand in front of your leg as you ask the horse to move his right shoulder to the left, can you see what a conflict the horse might experience?

* Aids should be of the optimum intensity. They should be applied strongly enough to be effective yet not too strong or they might frighten the horse or develop resistance in him. One of the goals of training is to get a horse to respond to lighter and lighter aids. When you need a greater response from your horse, do not automatically use a more forceful aid but instead a more effective aid. An abrupt, well-placed bump with the lower leg rather than a steady squeeze will often get the response you want.

Use your aids lightly and increase them as needed. If a horse doesn't respond to a natural aid, you can use an artificial aid to reinforce it. (See the section on artificial aids that follows.) Whether you use a natural aid or an artificial aid, use it with only as much intensity as you can control. In other words, if you want your horse to move away from your right leg, apply the type and intensity of aid which will achieve a step sideways. If you inappropriately haul off and kick your horse in the right side with the heel of your boot, perhaps with a spur and maybe even with the addition of a whip, your horse will likely rush excitedly to the left and throw his head up. Now you have two things to correct. You have created a worse situation. You not only need to apply the aids with an appropriate intensity but also need to be ready with counter-balancing aids (in this case, the left rein and leg) to contain the horse's response and help to shape it into a desired form.

The more responsive you make a horse to your seat and legs, the lighter he will automatically become in the bridle because his body will have a sense of forward motion and impulsion. If your driving aids are applied correctly, your horse will carry his head in a naturally pleasing configuration that does not have to be altered with rein aids but can instead be lightly guided into position.

* Aids should always be followed soon (within a second) by a reward or release for the horse when he complies with your wishes. If you ask a horse to slow down by deepening your seat and closing your hands on the reins and he slows down but you continue to hold him with your seat and hands, he has not been rewarded for doing as you asked. He continues to compact and gets tense. If you make this rider error several times in a row, the horse will lose the incentive to slow down for you in the future. Why bother? However, if you relax the aids slightly when your horse complies, he will not only be willing to repeat his behavior for you in the future, he will look forward to the aids that ask for it.

THE NATURAL AIDS

Your mind is a powerful force that helps you visualize, coordinate, evaluate, and modify all of your training activities. Your voice is a human means of communication, not as appropriate for riding training as it was for ground training, so your voice will be gradually de-emphasized.

The Seat
The foundation of good riding begins with a balanced, symmetric, following seat: Your pelvis must follow the motion of the horse's hind-

quarters in order to effectively influence his movement. In order to ride properly, you must be sitting on a saddle that allows you to do this.

Every style of riding has its own standard of elegance and correctness and your overall position will vary depending on the style of riding you pursue. But a basic, balanced seat is essentially the same for bareback riding, stock seat riding, and dressage, three types of riding that many riders enjoy. Variations of the basic, balanced seat are used for hunt seat, jumping, saddle seat, endurance riding, reining, and cutting.

There should be even weight on both seat bones; your legs should lie softly along the horse's sides; your stirrups even; your shoulders level and square with your head facing forward and your neck straight. There should be a straight line from your ear through your shoulder joint through your hip joint to the back of your heel.

If you perch forward on your crotch, your seat bones no longer have contact with the saddle. You might ride with a hollow back that destroys your balance and prevents you from effectively communicating with your horse through your seat. You will tend to always be ahead of the motion of your horse and you might be easily popped off over the horse's head or shoulder if he should stop suddenly.

If you sit too far back in your saddle, your back pockets are pressed against the cantle. There are two variations of this faulty seat: the easy-chair position and the braced-for-action position. In the easy-chair position, you may find yourself raising your thighs to an almost horizontal configuration which will bring your lower leg far forward so that you cannot possibly keep any weight in your heel. If you ride this way, you are merely a passenger and will have little hope in positively affecting a horse's movement. Since you are way behind the motion of the horse, you could easily be left behind in a cloud of dust if your horse moves forward suddenly or turns.

If you ride in a braced position, your legs are either stiff out to the sides and/or shoved forward with your feet pushing into the stirrups. If you ride this way, you will have difficulty communicating with your horse's back or following his motion. You will also have a greater risk of experiencing stress injuries due to your rigid position.

The Back and Upper Body
You can use your pelvis, lower back, and the weight of your upper body in a variety of ways ranging from a soft, light following contact of your

seat to a strong, still stiffening. In most situations, your back and pelvis (when viewed from the side) should be straight, never hollowed, rounded, or slumped. If your back is hollow, the base of your pelvis has moved backward, tipping you forward on your crotch. If your back is rounded, the floor of your pelvis has moved forward excessively and you have let your abdominal muscles collapse. This will cause you to sit on your pockets.

Your upper body should be straight without being stiff. Movement of your upper body backward or forward even one degree will greatly affect a horse's composite balance. Your shoulders should be parallel with the horse's shoulders; that is, when making a turn to the left your left shoulder should move slightly back while your right shoulder should move slightly forward. This puts you in a position to approximate the arcs of movement of the horse's front legs. When a horse is turning to the left, the arc of his left leg is smaller than that of his right leg. Some riders collapse their bodies on one side as they ride. This can greatly affect a horse's lateral development and could set you up for problems with your spinal column.

The Lower Legs

It is important that you apply leg aids with proper intensity in the appropriate location on your horse's side. For most styles of riding, you can accomplish this best by letting your thighs relax and allowing your lower leg to maintain light, steady contact with your horse's side. If you actively try to use the muscles of your thighs for leg aids, you will probably create muscle tension that will push you up out of the saddle and cause you to have a loose seat.

In general terms, you will use your lower legs actively, passively, or in a yielding fashion. When you want a horse to move, whether it is forward, backward, or sideways, you use an active leg to aid your seat and hands in creating the desired motion. An active leg aid can consist of a squeeze, light bump, kick, or spur.

When you want a horse to continue the motion you have created, you use a passive leg unless the horse becomes sluggish and needs a reminder or until you wish to change what the horse is doing. A passive leg has contact with the horse's side but is not trying to actively change things.

A yielding leg is sometimes temporarily used when teaching a horse a new movement. For example, for a turn on the forehand, if you want your horse to move away from your right leg and the horse is confused, it might help initially if you took your left leg off the horse so as to create a space for him to move into. When you temporarily take your leg off a horse's side, you have used a yielding leg. Eventually, you will want your horse to move away from the right leg with your left leg passively in place.

Traditionally, leg aids are talked of in terms of at, in front of, or behind the girth or cinch; this is actually a misnomer. If you look at the leg of a balanced rider in its normal position, it is almost always *behind* the actual girth or cinch. (Photo 12 well illustrates this position.) You

12. The leg in the so-called "middle position" is actually behind the girth or cinch.

wouldn't want the girth or cinch between your leg and the horse's side anyway. So the standard leg position should be thought of as the middle position, which is actually somewhat behind the girth or cinch. This is the leg position that will initiate and maintain forward movement in a straight line. When you introduce turning or lateral movements or try to straighten the natural crookedness of a horse, you will have to begin using your legs in different positions.

When turning a horse, often your inside leg (inside referring to the inside of the arc of the turn) is used with moderate activity in the middle position to cause the curling reflex previously noted and to give the horse a point of reference around which to turn. As you turn, for example to the right, your right leg would serve as this "post" for the horse to turn around. If your horse when turning to the right arcs evenly from head to tail, then your left leg would also be in the middle position, but it would be either passive or very lightly active to maintain forward movement. If, however, your horse, as most young horses do, deviates in the turn or is resistant, you will have to adjust him with various positions of your legs.

If he swings his hips off to the left as he turns to the right, you can move your left leg behind the middle position to encourage him to carry his hindquarters up underneath himself in the turn rather than letting them lazily and sloppily swing out to the left side. If he is stiff in the shoulders and resists bending to the right as you turn, you can encourage him to pick his shoulders up and move them over by using your left leg in front of the middle position. Or if he resists in an almost disobedient fashion by a shoulder out to the left, you may have to back up your left leg in front of the middle position with the help of a whip held in front of your leg.

The outside leg will be especially important during turning maneuvers such as corners, circles, half-turns and serpentines. If your outside leg comes off your horse's side (which can very easily happen), you lose your balance, the horse loses a point of boundary reference, and his hindquarters can easily fall to the outside of the turn. This will further cause you to lose contact between your outside seat bone and the saddle and will allow a horse to drop his inside shoulder. Especially after a sharp turn, your outside leg may tend to slip forward and you will need to expend some energy to keep it back in position to act as a forward driving and holding aid. This is critical in a canter, for example, so you can keep the hindquarter in position in relation to the front end. If your legs consistently come off your horse, perhaps your stirrups are too long. If you find yourself losing contact with the saddle, perhaps your stirrups are too short, causing you to stand in them.

The Hands

Even though you should learn to de-emphasize the rein aids and maximize the effects of the leg, back, seat and mind, a knowledge of the rein aids is essential. The beauty of training a horse to respond to a progressive and logical system of rein aids is that when you have a trouble spot in a more complex maneuver, you will have a place to go back to review. This is reason alone to take the time to teach your horse the basics. In addition, using a sequence gives you a better chance for shaping your horse, not only having him perform the maneuver but also in balanced form.

This discussion of the rein aids pertains to work in a snaffle bridle or bosal. A snaffle bit may have a solid or broken mouthpiece. The reins create a direct pull on the corners of the horse's mouth, the tongue, and the bars. If a bit has shanks, no matter what the configuration of the mouthpiece, it operates with leverage as it exerts pressure between the chin groove and poll and therefore it is not a snaffle.

A horse's mouth is extremely sensitive and any fear of the bit or rigidity in the jaw will be reflected in the whole horse. That is why all of your rein aids must be applied with smoothness and finesse (photo 13). Fast jabs just make a horse tense and substantiate his fears about the bit. Uneven reins give incorrect signals.

13. Because a horse's mouth is extremely sensitive, the hands should be carried and used precisely and with finesse.

For all styles of riding, there must be some degree of contact. A too-tight rein never allows a horse to be rewarded so it is very unlikely that he will ever relax and move naturally. With all rein aids, a taking of the rein should be followed by a yielding if the horse responds correctly. You should release the aid somewhat and follow the horse's correct movement if even for a moment before reapplying the aids to remind and rebalance him. A yielding should be a subtle softening, not a total release of contact or you will lose the balance you gained by applying the aids in the first place. If the horse has responded incorrectly, you can either release the aid momentarily and reapply it or increase the aid and hold it until the horse responds to it. The latter should be practiced only by an experienced horseman and it is used so that a horse learns he must submit to the aids. It is crucial to follow the holding method with an immediate yielding upon compliance so that the horse develops the incentive to do the right thing.

A too-loose rein is usually neither safe nor effective. When rein cues are applied on a too-loose rein, they will probably require large movements on your part as you gather up your reins. Often such grand motions are felt as big surprises in the horse's mouth. It is better to have moderate contact, no matter what the style of riding, so that you can feel the horse and influence him with subtle movements of your hands. For rein aids to be most effective, they should be applied so there is a direct line from your elbow through your hand to your horse's mouth. Be very cautious about adopting (show ring) fads related to contact and rider arm position. Stick to the classic guidelines and you can't go wrong.

Be sure you do not overemphasize the rein aids. Rein aids should be subtle and should augment or add to the performance that is created by the more powerful aids: the mind, the seat, the upper body, and the legs. The reins should never be used to balance your upper body or stabilize your seat. Your hands must develop a steadiness independent from your other body movements.

The Action of the Rein Aids
The three basic rein aids are the leading rein, the direct rein, and the indirect rein.

The leading rein (or opening rein) is the most basic rein aid. In a right turn, you move your right arm out to the side and ask the horse to follow his nose (as seen in photo 14). There should be no backward force

14. The right leading rein using a bosal.

exerted on the rein. A right leading rein throws the horse's weight to the right foreleg, makes him temporarily "lose his balance," and causes him to try to regain his balance by moving to the right.

If the right leading rein opens the door, the left rein should give to allow the horse to go through the doorway. Without using any other aids, a right leading rein tends to swivel the horse on his middle. If you use a right opening rein and a left giving rein and do nothing more (no leg or weight cues), a horse will turn right with his weight on his forehand, a flat spine, and perhaps with his hindquarters swinging left — which is a perfectly acceptable way of going for the first few lessons. However, you do not want to use this rein-only approach too long or the undesirable accompanying body configuration will become a habit.

The leading rein, however, is an essential beginning step because it asks in uncomplicated terms for the horse to tip his nose down and into the direction of movement. If your hand is met with resistance, light intermittent tugs (tremors) will tend to break up the tension more effectively than an all-out tug-of-war or heavy steady pressure.

It is really only appropriate to use this rein aid at the walk and trot in the horse's early training. (By the time the horse is balanced at these gaits, he will be ready to move on to the direct rein and some work at the lope.) At the trot or jog, you will have to begin limiting the bend of your horse by changing the giving outside rein into a passive rein—that is, very light contact to regulate the bend, introduce vertical flexion, speed control, and regulation of circle size. You don't want to use a supporting outside rein too early because it would confuse the horse to feel conflicting pressure on both sides of his mouth at once. After a few weeks of work using the leading rein, you should introduce the direct rein so that you can begin adding a supporting outside rein to the turns.

The direct rein is used in a number of combinations to shape your horse vertically and laterally. The direct rein is a contact straight from the horse's mouth through your hand toward your hip. A right direct rein settles the weight of the horse to his right shoulder or toward his right hip. (See photo 15.)

When you exert equal holding or backward pressure with both reins you are said to be using bilateral direct rein of opposition (as shown in photo 16). This, along with appropriate driving aids, opposes the mass and energy of the hindquarters to the mass and energy of the forehand and eventually results in what is referred to as vertical (longitudinal) flexion and ultimately to collection. Your long-term goal is for your horse to work with this physical organization in all of his movements. The direct rein is one of the important keys to help you achieve this energy balance. But with a young horse, the application of the direct rein should always be very light, allowing him to develop free, forward movement.

When tracking straight (up the long side of the arena, for example, or down a straight road), you will be catching your horse between your aids. You should feel an elastic connection between your right leg and seat bone and the right rein and between your left leg and seat bone and the left rein. The direct rein will also serve to hold the horse's body in left to right balance as you perform turns. At first, the rein contact is very light; gradually both the driving aids and direct rein contact is increased.

An indirect rein aid is applied on one side of the horse but affects, predominantly, the other side of the horse. The effect is generally in the form of a weight shift and/or a change in the direction of travel. Indirect rein aids are used in lateral movements—shoulder-in, two-track, turn on

15. The right direct rein using a bosal.

16. Bilateral direct rein with a slight bend to the left.

the hindquarters (haunches), and sidepass, to name a few. The indirect rein for the most part is too advanced for the young horse but its use should be understood so that it is not used prematurely.

The two indirect reins are called the indirect rein of opposition in front of the withers and the indirect rein of opposition behind the withers. If a leading rein is described as an opening to the side and a direct rein as a straight backward/forward contact, then an indirect rein could be called a sideways shift.

Your hand should not cross to the opposite side of the horse's neck, but instead should move toward your opposite shoulder or hip. Depending on the action of the other rein and other rider aids (and the level of training of the horse), the indirect rein can be used to help bend the horse and shift his weight from one side to another.

The indirect rein in front of the withers shifts the horse's weight from the shoulder on the side where the rein aid is applied to the other. The rein moves slightly backward and toward the withers but does not cross over the withers. This rein aid is used in the turn on the forehand and the leg-yield.

The indirect rein behind the withers shifts the horse's weight from one shoulder to the opposite hind leg. The rein is held behind the withers and moves toward the rider's opposite hip but does not cross the midline of the horse. This rein aid is part of the aid sequence for teaching a horse a turn on the hindquarters.

To make the difference between the two indirect rein aids clear, picture an extreme indirect rein in front of the withers, midway down your horse's neck and contrast that with an extreme indirect rein behind the withers, for example, in the vicinity of the pommel or swells of your saddle. All other aids being equal, the first example would shift the horse's weight to the opposite shoulder, and the second example would shift the weight to the entire opposite side of the horse but particularly the opposite hindquarter.

Once the weight is shifted to a particular "quarter" of the horse's body, you then need to tell the horse to either hold the weight there or keep the weight moving in that direction. If you want the horse to settle the weight on a particular leg, you are stabilizing a pivot foot—for example, as in a turn on the forehand or a turn on the hindquarter. You would help your indirect rein aid (which has sent the weight where you want it) with a light supporting direct rein to impede forward movement. You would need to use the appropriate leg aid to ask the horse to step sideways. Also, a slight shift of your weight toward the target quarter will further stabilize the leg.

If, on the other hand, you want the horse's weight to continue moving toward a particular quarter or side, you must adjust your aids. For example, in a leg-yield or two-track, where the horse is moving on an oblique (both forward and sideways), it is important not to restrain his forward movement as was necessary in the situation of stabilizing a pivot foot. The supporting rein must be more giving in its contact and you must create the forward motion through cues by your back, seat, and legs. Your weight should be used toward the direction of movement.

Forms of the indirect rein are used to neck rein western horses. On sharp turns (the turn on the hindquarters) the western rider elevates his hand slightly to settle the weight on the hindquarters (photo 17) but the signal to turn comes from the rein on the horse's neck, the rider's weight shift, and leg aids. For more gradual turns, such as when circling, the hand is held low and steady and the weight of the rein against the horse's neck is the cue for the horse to arc his body and turn.

The neck rein is really more of a conditioned reflex than a rein aid. The horse is taught to turn away from the touch of the rein on its neck: When the rein touches the right side of the neck, the horse turns left. The horse has been taught by the rider first using two hands: One applies an

17. For sharp turns and other collected moves, the western rider picks up the reins slightly to settle the weight on the hindquarters.

opening rein and the other applies an indirect rein. To teach the horse to turn to the left, a left opening rein is applied slightly before the right indirect rein. Gradually, the time between the two rein aids is decreased. Also, the intensity of the left opening rein is diminished until the horse turns left simply from the touch of the right rein on his neck. A neck rein is most effective when it is applied just ahead of the withers.

A neck rein must be applied very lightly or it will give the horse the opposite signal than is desired. A strong right neck rein would actually pull the horse's nose to the right and backward which would put the horse in an awkward configuration for turning left. If you find yourself tempted to use this much rein in an attempt to neck rein to the left, one or two things need work. Either the horse needs a review lesson or you need to learn how to use more effectively your seat and legs to assist you in turning the horse so you can de-emphasize your rein aids.

The Role of the Outside Rein

The supporting action of the outside rein serves many purposes. Using the example of the left rein being the outside rein on a turn to the right (illustrated in photo 18):

---

* It prevents the horse from overbending to the right.
* It maintains the degree of vertical flexion and collection that was in evidence on the straightaway.
* It helps to hold up the inside (right) shoulder, or at least prevents the horse's weight from dropping onto the inside shoulder.
* It helps regulate the size and shape of the turn or circle.

In most cases, the outside rein is a stabilizing force. It provides your horse with a constant point of reference as to the gait, speed, and degree of collection in which he should be performing. In general terms, the outside rein should be steady so your horse can relax both mentally and physically as evidenced by a softness in his jaw, poll, and neck. If the outside rein is kept steady, a horse realizes that the rein will always be there and he will conform his mental attitude and the frame of his body to that reference point. If the outside rein is too loose, your horse will likely experiment with falling on his forehand, dropping to the inside,

18. The outside rein
serves many
purposes including
preventing the horse
from overbending
and falling on the
inside shoulder.

or letting his outside shoulder bulge through the outside rein. On the other hand, if the outside rein is too tight, the horse will likely be tense, either come above the bit or behind the bit, or counter-flex (bend his head in the opposite direction of the turn).

The connection to the outside rein should be from your outside hip bone, through your elbow, wrist and hand, through the rein to the lips or bars of the horse's mouth. This boundary that you have created contains your horse's energy and, depending on the degree of your driving aids, gives the horse a specific parameter for the degree of energy and engagement with which he must perform. And yet this boundary should not be rigid or unyielding; it should be characterized by a giving hand that yields to the horse in rhythm with his movement. The outside rein should never be "thrown away" during active work or the horse loses his point of reference for balance and collection. The exceptions to this are when testing the thoroughness of a horse's training or when allowing a horse a stretch break.

The Role of the Inside Rein
The inside rein can be used steadily or in a subtle, fluid, massaging way to get your horse's attention, to develop bending and flexion, and to shape your horse's form in various maneuvers. Its use should be in harmony with the outside rein. The more you use your seat, upper body, and legs, the less pronounced the action of the inside rein will need to be.

The inside rein is often slackened for a moment or two when the horse is performing in a desired state to test the self-carriage of the horse: Is the horse holding himself in the desirable configuration on his own or is he is dependent on the rider's aids to keep him together? The stronger and more physically developed a horse is, the more he is capable of self-carriage.

In general, do not hold aids. Use an aid, get the desired response, and return to the neutral position. Taking with the reins must always be followed by a release so a horse's lightness is preserved and the horse is encouraged to work in self-carriage as soon as possible. Otherwise you will always have to hold him or force him to do things.

Do not pick at a horse by nagging him with the aids. Tell him what he can or cannot do according to his level of training and expect his compliance. If you nag with aids, the horse can become unresponsive or irritated.

As you introduce different maneuvers, at first, you can make the intensity and sequence of the aids exaggeratedly different from previously learned maneuvers so the young horse can clearly tell the difference. Eventually, however, you will want to gradually alter the aids so that they all are delivered subtly and in a standard fashion.

Constantly remind yourself to de-emphasize rein aids. Otherwise a horse may get behind the bit, the very worst of all tendencies to fix. A great number of problems are eliminated when a horse is encouraged and allowed to move forward more freely. If a horse gets tense and bunched up, he can create all sorts of imperfections in his movement. When you feel this happening, rather than trying to fix things with clever manipulations of your hands, line the horse out, drive him forward, push the GO button, however you want to say it—*just get the horse moving forward and many of your problems will be left behind in the dust.*

3

Tack

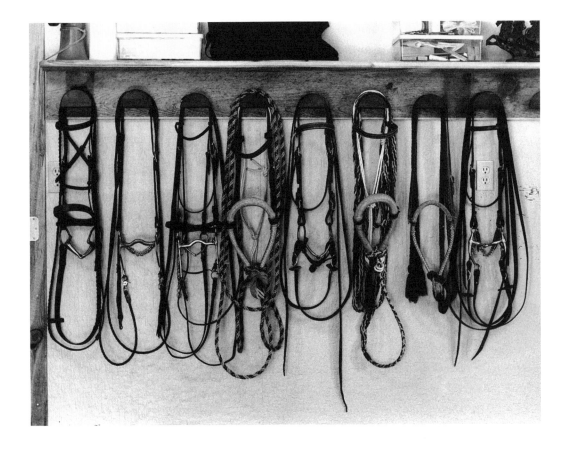

Western Saddles

There are many features to consider when selecting a western saddle for training. The tree, the framework on which the saddle is built, should be chosen for strength and proper fit.

The slope and shape of the seat is a result of the "ground work" that is added over the tree. Saddle makers add plates of rawhide or metal and layers of leather to achieve the desired seat style from very flat to deeply cupped or highly contoured high-rise fronts.

Some so-called equitation saddles have an extremely built-up front to the seat which supposedly locks a rider in the proper position. However, such a saddle does not allow a rider to shift her weight forward and backward as needed for training. Your best bet is to use a saddle with a balanced, versatile seat—one that is relatively flat and deep with a moderately high cantle. Moderate to full swells will provide you with security while you are training. The horn should be set low and the horn cap moderate to wide so that if you are thrown forward, you won't get a sharp blow from the horn.

Some trainers prefer oxbow stirrups because they stay hooked on a rider's foot during a storm. Others recommend a moderately wide and heavy stirrup so it can easily be kicked free during a mishap. Choose according to your skill level and inclination.

There are two popular ways of attaching the rigging to the saddle. Ring rigging consists of large, flat rings suspended from leather straps that are securely attached to the tree. The latigo cinch strap or half breed is fastened to the cinch ring. While ring rigging makes a very strong saddle because the ring and latigo are located under the rider's leg, the bulk can interfere with subtle communication between the rider's leg and the horse's side. To counter this, skirt rigging has become popular. Skirt rigging consists of a metal plate or a reinforced leather slot located at the bottom of the saddle skirt (photo 19). Bulk is reduced and so could the strength of the rigging if poor quality skirting leather is used. The slots in the plates used in skirt-rigged saddles will allow you to vary the position of the saddle on the horse's back. This adaptability is not possible with ring rigging.

Front cinches are made of mohair, cotton, or synthetic fibers. Cinches range in length from 22 to 36 inches; the average is 30 to 32 inches. Hardware on the cinches should be solid stainless steel or brass.

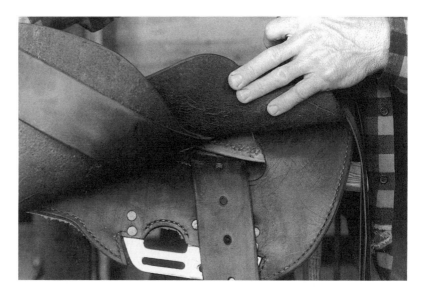

Forged metals are much stronger than cast ones. Chrome-plated
hardware is less desirable. Two small D-rings are sewn at the middle
of a western cinch. One is for the attachment of the rear cinch
connecting strap, and the other provides a point of connection for a
breast collar or martingale. If you use a rear cinch, be sure to accustom
your young horse to it during longeing and be sure to use a rear cinch
connecting strap to prevent the cinch from sliding back to the flank.
Bypassing either of these steps could result in your horse bucking when
you ride him.

English Saddles

English saddles are built on either rigid or spring trees. The rigid wooden
tree found in older saddles has little give and results in a stiff seat. The
spring tree, most popular today, has two spring steel plates which run
the length of the wooden bars. These plates yield to the pressures of
weight and movement, so result in some shock absorbency and greater
comfort for both the rider and the horse. Spring trees characteristically
have deeper seats than rigid trees.

The head of the English saddle is the portion of the pommel above the
withers of the horse. The head may be vertical, sloped back, or cut back

to accommodate various types of withers. A vertical head might fit an Arabian with low withers but may bruise a Thoroughbred with prominent withers. The Thoroughbred may require a saddle which has the ceiling of the head cut back, allowing the withers to protrude. A cutback saddle is good for the trainer who works horses with varying types of withers.

Stirrup bars are metal brackets by which the stirrup leathers are attached to the saddle. Most have a safety latch, which will allow the stirrup leather to slip away from the saddle in the case of an accident. Forged steel stirrup bars are preferred because of superior strength. The position of the stirrup bars dictates the position of the stirrup leathers and consequently the rider's leg, so check to be sure that the position will be appropriate for your style of training.

The panels, the stuffing on the underside of the saddle, are the bearing surface that distributes your weight over your horse's back. Panels come in various shapes which cover differing amounts of surface area. The stuffing of the panels should be examined for evenness and symmetry.

Some dressage saddles have knee rolls or thigh rolls to stabilize the position of the rider's leg. Saddles for hunters and jumpers almost always have knee rolls to keep the rider from moving forward off the saddle while negotiating a jump. Close contact saddles which are primarily used for eventing usually have no rolls.

Girths may be string, web, or leather. String and web girths are less expensive and can be easily washed but are not as durable as contoured leather girths with elastic buckle straps. Stirrup leathers should be smooth, close-grained and durable without being too thick. When choosing stirrup leathers, avoid those made of stretchy leather.

Use a standard stainless steel iron with ample room for your boot. Tread widths are available in the 4.5- to 5-inch range. Rubber stirrup pads are an option which increase grip and stirrup security.

Fitting the Saddle to the Horse

How well the saddle fits the horse is extremely important with young horses and is determined by the dimensions of the tree on which the saddle is built. Most saddles, both English and western, come in the same general tree types. The wide tree (called full Quarter Horse in western saddles) is designed for a horse with heavy, low withers and a well-muscled back. The medium tree (semi-Quarter Horse or warmblood) fits a horse with moderately high and narrow withers and medium muscling of the back. The Arabian tree has flat, short bars to fit the wide, short back of the Arabian. English saddles are also available in very narrow (sometimes called Thoroughbred) trees to accommodate the horse with very thin, tall withers and a rafter back.

The gullet must be tall enough to allow a mounted rider to put three fingers between the saddle and the horse's withers. The width of the gullet (being measured in photo 20) must allow a saddle to ride balanced from front to rear without rolling forward and pinching the withers or tipping back and loading the loin. The rider's weight is transferred to the horse through the bearing surface of the saddle, that part which contacts the horse's back. There must be an appropriate space between the bars to fit the width of the horse's back. A saddle with bars too close together for a wide-backed horse will perch on top of the horse's back rather than nestling down on it. The angle and twist of the bars should allow the saddle to lay uniformly all along the horse's back for an even weight distribution. When the maximum bearing surface of the saddle distributes the rider's weight evenly over the back muscles, the horse is most comfortable. A western saddle has a larger bearing surface than an English saddle, so is more appropriate for training young horses, especially those with sensitive or undeveloped backs.

20. Measuring the gullet of a fairly standard dressage saddle.

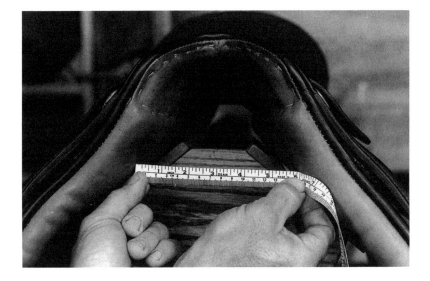

The sweat marks under a properly fitted saddle are usually symmetric and the hair is slick. The ill-fitting saddle will leave dry spots (saddle was very tight or made strong contact) or ruffled hair (saddle moved around) on the horse's back. Weight concentrated on a particular area of the back may cause pain and subsequent irritation and resistance from the horse. Ill-fitting saddles often result in spots of white hair.

The length of the bars should correspond to the length of the horse's back. Short-backed, close-coupled horses, such as Arabians and some Quarter Horses, require saddles with shorter bars and perhaps rounded skirts instead of long, square skirts. Forcing a short-backed horse to wear a long saddle can cause soreness in his loin area, imbalance the saddle forward, thus resulting in a disproportionate amount of the rider's weight to be borne at the withers, or cause the skirts to poke the horse's hip bones. Using a too-short saddle on a long-backed horse would not allow the rider to sit in the optimum position for effective riding.

To see if a saddle fits, set the saddle, without any pads, on the horse's back and check from the front and rear for wither and backbone clearance. Try to rock the saddle from front to back and from side to side. The saddle that fits like a glove will be difficult to move. It is as if there is a suction created between the horse's back and the underside of the saddle.

Western saddles can be measured in several places. In the gullet, the distance between the areas directly under the saddle strings is the gullet width. Most horses require a 6-inch to 7-inch-wide gullet.

With the aforementioned line as an imaginary horizontal axis, measure the distance up to the bottom of the gullet. This vertical line can be thought of as the height of the gullet. The average horse needs about a 2.5-inch-high gullet. Thoroughbred-type withers may require up to 4- or 5-inches for clearance.

English saddle fit can be estimated in a similar fashion measuring between the points of the bars then continuing as outlined for western saddles. Choosing a saddle that is too wide or too low in the gullet with the intention of adding extra blankets to rectify the situation is not wise. Adding more padding just puts you farther away from the horse and makes more bulk between your aids and the horse. It also makes the saddle unstable and makes it easier for you to shift off center. Besides, the saddle still fits improperly; the pressure has just been transferred and possibly intensified by the addition of the thick layers.

Bridles

A number of different kinds of bridles are available (See photo 21) for your training goals.

THE SNAFFLE

The snaffle bit is the most appropriate bit for early riding. It acts only with direct pressure so it delivers a simple signal to the horse's mouth. There are no shanks, therefore no leverage is involved. The mouthpiece of a snaffle can be jointed or solid. The misconception that any bit with a jointed mouthpiece is a snaffle has given rise to the misnomers "long-shanked snaffle," "cowboy snaffle," and "tom-thumb" snaffle, all of which are really jointed curbs. Any bit with shanks is classified as a curb.

Factors That Affect Snaffle Bit Action
* The rider's hands
* The configuration of the mouthpiece: jointed or solid
* The thickness of the mouthpiece
* The weight of the mouthpiece
* The texture of the mouthpiece
* The type of metal of the mouthpiece
* The types of rings or cheeks
* The width of bit
* The adjustment of the bridle (and noseband if used)

A rider's hands have the capacity to turn the most mild bit into an instrument of abuse or the most severe bit into a delicate tool of communication. Above all, good horsemanship is the key to a horse's acceptance of the bit. So that your horse thoroughly accepts contact with the bit, you must use all of your aids effectively to gain compliance from the horse's entire body; remember, you must yield when he complies.

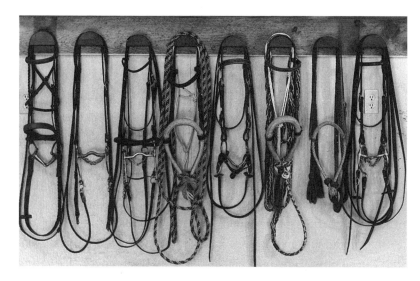

21. Choose the bridle most appropriate for your training goals.

A snaffle's mouthpiece can be solid or jointed. Jointed mouthpieces are preferred over solid mouthpieces for suppling and lateral work such as bending and turning. A bit with "loose action" (movement of the arms, both at the joint and at the rings) will encourage your horse to "mouth" the bit, to roll it and lift it with his tongue. This mouthing leads to suppleness and relaxation in his jaw. A jointed mouthpiece naturally provides tongue relief because the bit can peak over the tongue. The curvature of the arms will also affect the comfort and effectiveness of the bit. Curved arms will better conform to a horse's tongue while straight ones can press on and restrict it.

A solid mouthpiece provides more stopping power than a jointed bit of equal thickness because it maintains a steady pressure on the tongue. But a horse can brace against a solid bit causing him to stiffen his jaw. A straight, solid mouthpiece rests directly on the sensitive bars and does not allow enough space for a horse's tongue to function comfortably. A mullen (slightly bowed) mouthpiece provides more tongue and bar relief. (See photos 22 and 23.)

The thickness of a mouthpiece is measured one inch from the rings. Mouthpieces 3/8 inch or thicker are generally used to start young horses. The thicker the mouthpiece, the larger the surface area that receives pressure from the rein aid; the pressure is transmitted to a larger area, therefore the sensation is milder. If a horse tends to get behind the bit (flexing his poll so his head is behind the vertical), changing to a thicker mouthpiece may encourage him to take contact. However, a too-thick

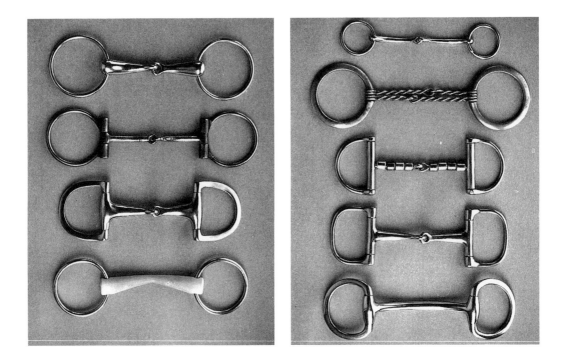

22. (above left) Common training snaffles from top: standard smooth mouthed, stainless steel o-ring; cold-rolled steel (with copper inlays) Don Dodge; stainless steel D-ring; solid mouth "rubber" bar.

23. (above right) Snaffle variations: stainless steel Bradoon; nickel alloy double-twisted wire; copper and stainless roller D-ring; standard stainless D-ring; mullen mouth eggbutt.

mouthpiece (like a 3/4-inch straight "hot dog" rubber bit) can gag a small-mouthed horse. Thin mouthpieces (less than 3/8 inch) press sharply into the nerves that lie just below the skin of the tongue and bars and can cause pain and tension in a young horse's mouth.

Thick mouthpiece snaffles generally weigh more because of the additional material required to make them. This can be an advantage because weight stabilizes the bit in a horse's mouth. But thick, heavy bits can also result in dull reactions and a very low-head carriage from some horses. If a horse doesn't respond to a thick bit, provided all of your other aids are adequate, it may be beneficial to try a thinner bit. Hollow bits are available for horses that work well in a thick mouthpiece but do not carry themselves well with a heavy bit.

The texture of the mouthpiece can be smooth, wavy, ribbed, ridged, or rough. For early training, a smooth mouthpiece is most appropriate. It slides through a horse's mouth uneventfully, so there are no surprises and he can react fluidly and without tension. In contrast, an uneven surface bumps the horse's mouth as the bit moves from side to side. This can serve to get a horse's attention or make him afraid. If a horse is injured by a bit, he may avoid contact with it by getting behind the bit or tossing his head in an effort to escape contact.

Textured mouthpieces, such as a slow twist (a thick mouthpiece with three or four twists), a scrub board (with built-up strips in the mouthpiece), a wire-wrap, or a twisted-wire snaffle are designed to lighten up a tough-mouthed horse and don't have a place in standard training of young horses.

The material of the mouthpiece can affect your horse's sensitivity to it. Saliva is a sensitivity enhancer. Nerve impulses, tiny electrical transmissions, are more efficiently sent through moist tissue. The production of saliva increases when the parotid glands are stimulated due to flexion at the jaw and poll. This flexion, along with an overall balance and suppleness in your horse's movement, gets the saliva flowing (see photo 24), but the bit you put in his mouth can either encourage or discourage his moist mouth.

Snaffles are commonly made of stainless steel, cold-rolled steel, or copper alloys. High-quality stainless steel has a bright, smooth, long-wearing surface that won't rust or pit. Stainless steel is considered a neutral in regards to salivation. Cold-rolled steel, or "sweet iron," is

24. A moist mouth is potentially a more receptive mouth. Salivation results from active forward work and flexion in the jaw and poll.

compressed to form a uniformly dense, yet softer, darker material than stainless. This metal is prone to rusting, but its fans think of the rust as "seasoning," maintaining that the nutmeg-colored oxidation on the mouthpiece makes it taste sweet, hence the nickname. True to its name, sweet iron encourages salivation. Show snaffles usually have cold-rolled steel mouthpieces but are referred to as silver bits because of the engraved silver inlaid on the rings.

Copper alloys, which have a reddish gold hue, are used for solid mouthpieces and as strips inlaid in cold-rolled steel or stainless steel mouthpieces. Copper enhances salivation but is a soft metal that can wear out and break from joint movement or develop sharp points if your horse chews the bit. Aluminum and chrome bits tend to dry out a horse's mouth. A rubber bit may seem kind but must be offensive to some horses because they try to spit the bit out.

25. (below left) Bit guards can be used to prevent skin pinching caused by flat ring snaffles.

26. (below right) Close-up of ring attachment of a ring snaffle and a D-ring snaffle.

Snaffle rings are usually made of flat stock or round wire. Round wire rings require much smaller holes in the mouthpiece than do flat rings. The large "loose" holes in a flat-ringed bit are notorious for trapping lip skin. Also as flat rings move, they wear the edges of the holes in the mouthpiece to form rough burrs which can rub skin raw. To prevent this, bit guards (shown in photo 25) are sometimes used with flat ring snaffles.

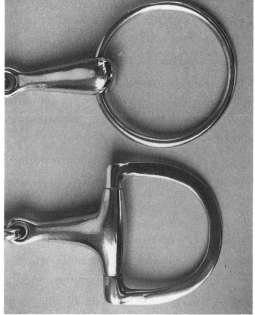

Some western snaffles are constructed with a sleeve at the junction of the mouthpiece that results in a tighter movement but minimizes skin pinching.

The rings of the snaffle put pressure on the sides of a horse's face and also help stabilize the bit in his mouth. Large rings (those over 4 inches) can apply pressure to sensitive areas on your horse's face, areas where there is virtually skin over bone. Rings that are too small (under 1 1/2 inches) do not provide enough surface contact and could slip into your horse's mouth and be pulled across his teeth during a turn. For optimum communication and stability, choose a snaffle with 3-inch rings.

Eggbutt and D-ring snaffles are usually constructed to avoid skin pinching. (Photo 26 illustrates the difference between a ring snaffle and a D-ring.) The swivel mechanism is located above and below the corners of the mouth. An eggbutt mouthpiece is more stable than an O-ring, subsequently less mobile. Some horses need a bit with looser action and some do better with a bit that has a more stable, fixed action. A D-ring snaffle (sometimes called a racing bit) has a stable action because of the vertical "cheek pieces" that are part of the D configuration.

A full cheek (Fulmer) snaffle comes with a prong (spoon) both above and below the mouthpiece of the bit. Half cheek snaffles have either a spoon above or below the bit. Spoons should not be confused with shanks as the reins do not attach to cheek spoons. The spoons provide added lateral persuasion; when a rider pulls a left rein, the spoons on the right side of the bit are pulled against the right side of the horse's face to encourage him to turn left. A full cheek snaffle cannot be pulled through a horse's mouth. Using specialized cheek piece loops with a full cheek snaffle assures that the mouthpiece will remain still and upright in the horse's mouth. This will cause the flatter part of the bit to be presented to the tongue and the bars, otherwise (without using the loops) the mouthpiece can roll forward, is unstable, and presents the narrow edge of the bit to the tongue and bars.

Fit of the Snaffle

In order for a snaffle to work effectively, it must fit the horse properly and be adjusted correctly. Figure 2 shows the fit in a two-year-old mouth. The width of the mouthpiece should allow the bit to extend 1/4 inch on each side of the horse's mouth. Bits narrower than this will have a tight

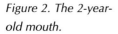

Figure 2. The 2-year-
old mouth.

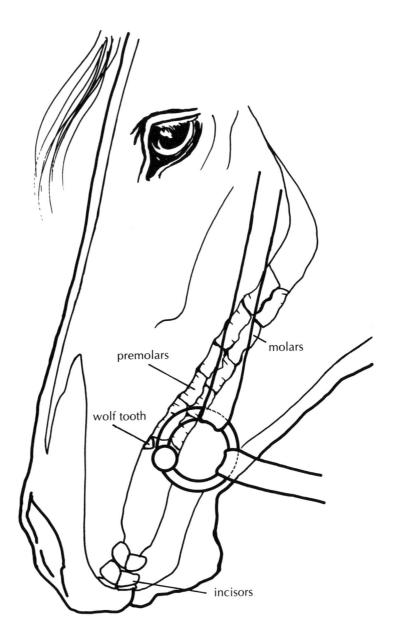

premolars

molars

wolf tooth

incisors

action and will likely cause skin pinching at the corner of the mouth.
Wider bits will hang in an inverted V on your horse's tongue and every
time you signal him with a rein, the V will have to straighten and the bit
will have to travel excessively through his mouth. The excess mechanical action will not only slow his reaction time, it will also make your

signals confusing to him. Standard snaffle width is 5 inches; some young horses require a narrower bit.

Adjust the headstall so that the snaffle just touches the corners of your horse's lips without causing wrinkles. If you look inside his mouth, you'll see that the bit lies in the interdental space and rests on his tongue and bars.

If the headstall is adjusted too tightly, the bit will exert constant pressure on the corners of the horse's mouth, leading to mental and physical dullness; there is no way for him to receive a release (reward) even when he is going just like you want him to.

Allowing the snaffle to hang too low might encourage a horse to put his tongue over the bit. And each time you pick up a rein, the bit will have to travel a considerable distance through the horse's mouth before it reaches the target area of communication. Traditionally, western horses are fitted with a looser headstall than English horses. The western horse is encouraged to pick the bit up with his tongue and carry it. The English horse, on the other hand, is fitted with a snugger headstall and ridden with a higher degree of rein contact. The goal is less movement of the bit in the horse's mouth. The English bit is further stabilized with the use of a noseband.

Sometimes a horse will become preoccupied with putting his tongue over the bit in an attempt to find more room for his tongue or to avoid the pressure of harsh hands on the bit. This habit can be avoided by using responsive hands and a properly fitted and adjusted bit. Further remedies include using a solid mouth snaffle or a noseband. When a noseband is used with a snaffle bit, it keeps the horse's mouth closed and stabilizes the bit which prevents the horse from avoiding the action of the bit. However, a too-tight noseband will not allow mouthing (quiet working and rolling of the bit on the tongue) of the bit. Remember, mouthing is desirable because it encourages the horse to relax his jaw.

Reactions to the Snaffle

A horse's reaction to pressure and/or pain in his mouth will depend on his past experiences with a bit and the current level of pressure or pain. Mild pressure tends to elicit submission or movement away from the stimulus; pain caused by strong pressure tends to elicit rebellion or movement into the pressure in an attempt to push through it to avoid the pain.

A young horse reacts very differently in a snaffle bit than does a schooled horse. The two-year-old initially carries his head high and nose out. The bit rests on and communicates almost entirely with the corners of the horse's mouth. The young horse will roll the bit around with his tongue, chew it, and open his mouth as if he is trying to spit it out (photo 27). These behaviors will decrease as the horse gradually accepts the bit. The horse with more schooling in the snaffle will flex vertically at the poll, lower his head and reach forward accepting the pressure of the mouthpiece on his tongue and bars.

THE BOSAL

The hackamore (an Americanization of the Spanish word *la jaquima*) is a bitless bridle comprised of a headstall, bosal, mecate, and in some instances, a rope fiador as seen in photo 28 and Figure 3. Mechanical hackamores with metal shanks and curb chains are not considered training equipment so are not discussed here.

The bosal is the heart of the hackamore. All bosals are similar but are available with variations. Most bosals are made of either rawhide or

27. (below left) When first bridled, this young horse acts as if he wants to spit the bit out.

28. (below right) A training bosal with browband headstall, rope fiador, and horse hair reins.

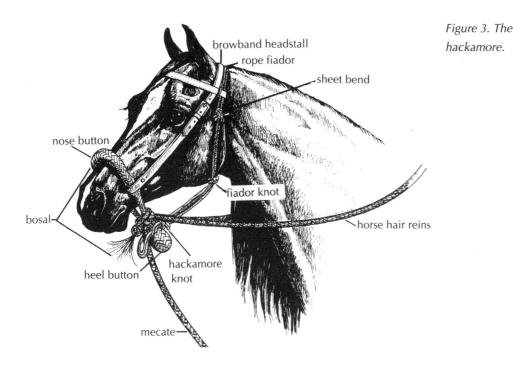

Figure 3. The hackamore.

browband headstall
rope fiador
sheet bend
nose button
fiador knot
bosal
horse hair reins
hackamore knot
heel button
mecate

latigo. Smoothness is affected by the number and size of the strands used to weave the bosal. A sixteen-plait bosal will generally be smoother and more expensive than one of eight plaits.

The core of a bosal gives it spring and flexibility. Cores are generally rawhide or cable. Rawhide cores vary in their stiffness and spring depending on how tight the rawhide inside is twisted. Rawhide core bosals can be soaked and then shaped with wooden forms to custom fit a horse's nose. Cable cores have some spring, but are relatively fixed and impossible to customize to an individual horse.

A bosal has four parts: the nose button, the side buttons, the cheek pieces, and the heel knot. The weight of the nose button and its subsequent effect is determined by its diameter and whether it is uniform in thickness or tapered. The side buttons are what keep the headstall in place. The size of a bosal is determined by the diameter of the cheek pieces. Training bosals are generally 5/8 to 3/4 inch while finishing-type "pencil" bosals are 3/8 to 1/2 inch. Sizes outside that range are not widely available. Heel knots come in various sizes and weights and should be of an appropriate weight to balance the bosal. The length of a bosal is measured on the inside from the heel knot to the nose button. The standard length is 12 inches.

Most bosals use a browband headstall about 1/2 inch wide. The browband needs to be adjustable or roomy enough to allow proper positioning and movement of the bosal. An excessively heavy or stiff headstall will inhibit the back and forth balancing movements of the bosal. A (non-adjustable) tight browband could cause the cheek pieces of the headstall to be pulled forward into the horse's eyes.

If the headstall has a roomy browband, a fiador will help keep the headstall's cheek pieces in position by exerting a backward pull on the browband. The fiador is optional and takes the place of the leather throatlatch that is often removed from the headstall. A fiador is made from about 16 feet of 1/4- or 5/16-inch-cotton or nylon sash cord which is doubled and knotted in a specific fashion. First, a hackamore knot is tied about 3 feet from the bight and then slipped over the heel knot of the bosal. The bight and the standing ends are joined and tied into a fiador knot. This is done so that the fiador knot ends up about 6 to 8 inches above the hackamore knot and rests just under the throat of the horse. The standing ends of the fiador are laced through the rear of the browband and tied on the near cheek to the bight with a sheet bend knot. These knots are best learned from an experienced horseman or from the pages of *How to Make Cowboy Horse Gear* by Bruce Grant.

The mecate, a 22-foot horse hair rope, comprises the reins and lead of the traditional hackamore. Ropes made of soft mane hair are preferred over coarser, more bristly tail hair. The prickly, errant hairs of a tail rope can be removed by a careful session with the electric clippers or a candle flame. Soaking stiff hair ropes in fabric softener usually helps to limber them up.

Mecates come in various diameters: 3/8 to 3/4 inch. For proper balance, use a 5/8-inch bosal with a 5/8-inch or narrower mecate.

The mecate is attached near the heel knot of the bosal using one to three wraps and a half hitch to secure the wraps. The number of wraps is determined when fitting the bosal to the horse's nose. You should be able to fit three fingers between the mecate wraps and the horse's jaw when you are finished. The excess weight caused by too many wraps can cause imbalance in the action of the bosal. If you make more than three wraps to attain the proper fit, you should consider finding a more appropriate bosal for your horse.

Somewhere between the first wrap and before the half hitch is made, the reins are pulled out of the top of the bosal. Using a length equivalent

to the distance between the hands when the arms are extended (a *brazada*) results in a rein length ending approximately 6 inches behind the horse's withers. This will allow the rider adequate slack for a comfortable hand position when working the horse.

The remainder of the horse hair rope, about 12 feet, serves as a lead. The lead is coiled and secured to the saddle strings or horn so that it does not interfere when the horse turns.

Properly fitted, the nose button of the bosal rests on the bridge of the nose with the cheek pieces of the bosal angling downward from the horizontal. This enables the rider to exert a lever action between the nose and the jaw as well as to reward the horse with release of pressure. When there is little or no contact with the reins, the cheek pieces rest about one inch above the corner of the horse's mouth and the bosal does not come in contact with the jaw bones. It is essential that the headstall, mecate wraps, and fiador, if used, are adjusted so that release of pressure is possible. If the hackamore is fitted too snug or too high up and exerts constant pressure on the nose and jaw, the horse will receive no reward for light, responsive behavior, and he could become unnecessarily bloody or calloused on the nose and jaw and mentally sour or dull.

The first reaction (reflex) a green horse usually has to a bosal is to push out against the pressure on the nose button and raise his head in response to the upward pressure of the cheek pieces on the jaw. However, it won't take long for the horse to learn to bring his head down to turn left and right if you continue to drive him forward and use light intermittent pressure and release with one rein at a time. Pressure should be used sparingly. Bumping with every stride would be like tugging on a snaffle with every stride—it would soon irritate the horse or cause him to be dull. Use the "honor system": correct a horse, then leave him alone so he can demonstrate for you his level of self-carriage (photo 29).

Bosals can excel over snaffles in vertical maneuvers such as stopping and backing, but must be used especially carefully when attempting lateral moves. Designed to respond to sideways pulls (opening rein) on the reins, a bosal can give somewhat confusing signals to the horse if the rider uses his hands straight backward (direct rein) for turning. A sideways pull of the right rein lays the left cheek piece on the side of the horse's face and says "turn your head to the right." A backward pull of the right rein can actually tip the horse's nose to the left at the same time a portion of the cheek piece says "turn right."

29. During first work in the bosal, a young horse typically will hold his head up and his nose out.

The location of the reins on the bosal can, to some degree, alleviate or aggravate this characteristic. When attaching the mecate, you will have the choice of bringing the reins out near the front wrap or at the heel knot. The former will assist you in bending your horse laterally while the latter is more effective for vertical flexion.

Be on the lookout for raw spots on your horse's nose and jaw. These are not necessary or desirable, and in fact are counterproductive. Sores are initially hypersensitive, then heal with thick scar tissue resulting in a loss of sensitivity. Wrapping the noseband with black electrical tape or the cheek pieces with sheepskin will help prevent sores, but better yet, move to a snaffle for a few weeks. Sensitive hands and good bosal fit are the ultimate safeguards.

Vertical moves such as stops and backs are often improved with the use of a hackamore. And, young horses that may be somewhat nervous with a snaffle often benefit from the relaxing effect of a bosal. The hackamore does not afford the rider as much control as does a snaffle, however, and does not provide the means to correct the horse's form in the precise way that a snaffle can. This means a bosal trainer must not be dependant on the bridle and must be capable of influencing the horse with other aids.

Other Equipment

Surcingle: A band of web or leather which encircles the horse's girth. A surcingle will have rings for various points of rein attachment and may have terrets through which driving lines can pass.

Longe line: 35-foot line that can be attached to a bridle or cavesson; on the other end a large loop handle or stops to help you hold onto the line.

Driving lines: 35-foot or longer lines of web, rope, or leather used in ground driving.

Side reins: Can be regular leather reins, reins with rubber donut inserts, nylon reins with elastic inserts, or reins with bunji cord incorporated in them.

Protective boots and bandages: Splint boots, bell boots, hind leg galloping boots (photo 30).

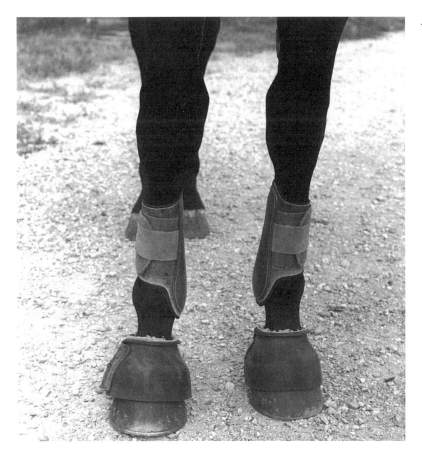

30. Protective boots.

Breast collar: Essential for hill work. The sensation of pressure (reflex) on a horse's chest may cause him to shorten his stride, stop, or even back up. A horse usually needs to become accustomed to a breast collar before he will work his shoulders freely with one in place.

ARTIFICIAL AIDS

Artificial aids are not necessary in the training of all young horses but may be helpful in some situations. They should be used to augment or reinforce your natural aids, never to replace them. You should design the use of an artificial aid to increase your chance of success by making things more clear and definite to a young horse, not frightening or confusing. Improper adjustment and crude or prolonged use of artificial aids are some of the most common causes of a sour mental attitude or the development of faulty movement.

The Whip

In the training of the young horse, a whip is more appropriate for creating forward movement than spurs. Use of the whip is based on the horse's reflex action of flexing the hind legs which is essential for forward movement. The use of spurs is based on the horse's reflex action of contracting the abdominals, which is a response more appropriate for collected work than forward work. A whip should be used with a light flick or touch, not a sharp cut or volley of stinging lashes. A horse must be calm and relaxed when you pick up and carry a whip as well as when you touch him with the whip. He should be attentive but not overly concerned and certainly not frightened or apprehensive. If a horse is tense at the sight of a whip he will tend to block the signals from the whip—his reflexes will not work. Therefore, a horse must learn that the whip is a tool, not a means of punishment. Rub the horse all over with the whip both from the ground and when mounted. A whip can be used humanely to heighten a lazy horse's response to the rider's legs which are asking the horse to move forward. A typical scenario involving the use of the whip to augment the leg might go like this:

1. The rider actively applies the lower legs. The horse does not respond. The rider's legs become passive.

2. The rider applies the lower legs, followed immediately by a tap

with the whip. The horse flexes the hind legs and moves forward with more energy. The rider's legs become passive.

3. The rider tests to see if the horse has learned.The rider applies the lower legs. The horse does not respond. The rider's legs become passive.

4. The rider reminds the horse that the whip will follow a lack of response. The rider applies the lower leg, followed immediately by a tap with the whip. The horse flexes the hind legs and moves forward more actively. The rider's legs become passive.

5. The rider tests again. The rider actively applies the lower legs. This time the horse flexes the hind legs and moves forward energetically.

A rider who uses the whip but no leg to develop forward movement has lost the effect of a very important tool. The horse may eventually become desensitized to the whip and the rider will have to use sharper and sharper cracks with the whip to get the horse's attention.

The whip should be thought of as a reinforcer not a replacer of the natural aids. That way the horse will remain responsive to it. A whip should never be used as punishment or in anger. It should be used with an effective tap, not a constant light nagging or an abusive series of intense raps. The whip should be used strongly enough so that the horse wants to avoid it but not so strongly that the horse becomes afraid. If the horse is afraid, he will not be relaxed and his reflexes will not work in a normal fashion. He will be mentally tense and unable to sort out what he is supposed to be learning.

A whip can be used in various positions to assist you. If a horse is falling in on his inside shoulder or bulging out on his outside shoulder, using the leg in front of the middle position on the offending side in conjunction with using the whip on the shoulder will signal the horse to carry himself upright and more balanced. Sometimes just holding a whip in the strategic position is enough of a reminder to the horse.

If a horse is not bending his body sufficiently for a circular movement, as I have shown in photo 31, using the whip just behind the girth will assist your inside leg in establishing and maintaining the bend in your horse's body. The whip can be used during turns on the forehand and leg-yielding to assist the rider's leg which is asking for sideways movement. The whip can be used on the outside to initiate a canter depart. Then the whip can be shifted to the inside to create and maintain

31. The whip can be used as a reinforcer, but should not be a replacer of the leg aids.

the bend during the canter. A tap with the whip on the horse's abdominal muscles tends to make him contract his abdominals which in turn causes him to arch his spine and bring his hind legs underneath his barrel.

A riding whip should be long enough to reach the horse's flank and hip without you having to move your hand backward to apply it. You might like to have whips in several lengths from 36 inches to 46 inches to accommodate different horses and training stages. A whip should feel well balanced in your hand; the longer a whip, the greater the tendency for the butt end to rotate upward and the tip to rotate downward. A well-designed whip often has a weighted end to help balance its length. And because you do not want to clench your fist as you ride, it is helpful if the whip has a cap which prevents the whip from sliding through and out of your hand.

The Running Martingale

Running martingales are frequently used in conjunction with snaffle bridles, but should not be used with curbs. A running martingale is Y-shaped. The base of the Y attaches to the cinch between the horse's front legs. The fork of the Y consists of two leather straps with rings on the ends; one strap works with each bridle rein. The reins pass through the martingale rings on the way from the bit to the rider's hands (photo 32). The running martingale is inactive until the horse raises his head. Then the downward pull created on the bit discourages further upward movement of the horse's head. Always use leather or rubber keepers (stops) on the reins when using a running martingale. They prevent the martingale rings from becoming hooked on the rein buckles or snaps which could cause the horse to panic.

A running martingale can allow you to ride your horse with a lighter rein while keeping him relatively straight and under control. This may be useful if a horse has a tendency to throw his head up repeatedly. It may also give you an added measure of safety control during some of your first cross country rides. Of course, be sure the horse is accustomed to the action of the running martingale long before you take him out. Adjust the action so that the rings of the martingale allow the reins to work in a straight line from the horse's mouth to your hands. If the rings are adjusted too low (short), the reins will act with a downward pull, forcing a horse to have an unnaturally low head position in front or carry

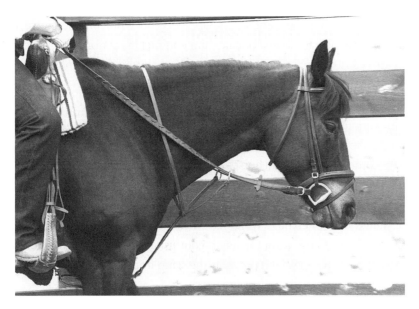

32. The running martingale should be adjusted so that it allows a horse to attain a natural head carriage. This horse's head could come up several inches before the running martingale is activated.

33. Spurs are appropriate for intermediate and advanced work and should be used to supplement the leg, not replace it.

his head behind the bit. A running martingale is a temporary training device and should not be used as a substitute for developing good hands.

Spurs

Since spurs are more appropriate for advanced work, it is unlikely you will use them in the early training of your young horse. When you decide it is time to use spurs, be sure you have a very steady seat and legs. Remember, spurs should augment the leg aids not replace them (illustrated in photo 33). If you apply the spur with a low, deep heel, it will cause the horse to round his back and move forward. If you jab the horse with a drawn up heel, it often causes a horse to hollow his back and to snap his hind legs upward but not necessarily reach them forward. Therefore, use your lower legs to drive your horse forward and the spur to collect him. Never use the spurs as a means of punishing a horse—it will only serve to drive a wedge between you and your horse. Since a properly applied left spur creates a collecting reaction in the left hind leg when it is pushing off, it would make no sense to use both spurs at the same moment during a walk or trot because it would be telling the right leg (in flight) to speed up which would be counterproductive to the collection desired. But in the canter, since both hind legs are essentially moving forward under the horse at the same time, using both spurs relatively simultaneously would be more logical.

4

Reviewing the Ground Rules

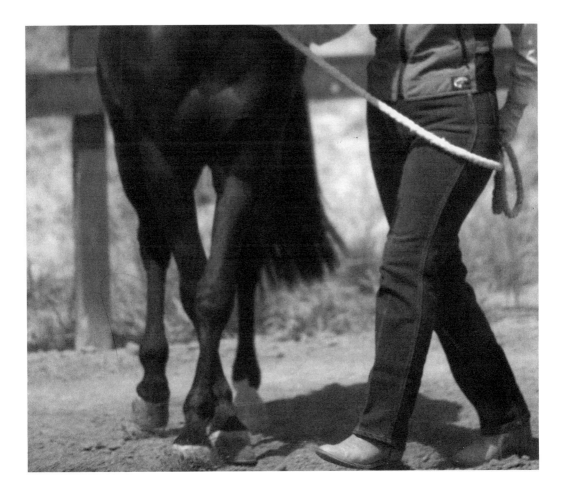

Preparation

Facilities. Training facilities need to be constructed for safety and strength. A horse's unpredictability and power are often underestimated. Horses should be tied at or above the level of the withers to a very stout post. It only takes one experience with breaking a rail and dragging the fragmented piece behind him in a frenzy to make a horse a life-long skeptic about being tied. It is ideal to have an outdoor tie area where you can let your horse stand tacked up for several hours each day (see photo 34). This does wonders for developing patience and a working attitude. Training a horse in an enclosure with flimsy fences is asking for trouble. The first time the horse is pressured into accepting your rules, he may take out a section of fence and in the process injure himself and you.

Round Pen: A pen 66 feet in diameter (20 m) will be suitable for longeing, driving, and riding. Smaller pens are not suitable for more than the first few rides. The round pen should have sloping walls (photo 35) about 7 feet tall with a base to hold in your footing. (See Hill, *Horsekeeping on a Small Acreage* for complete round pen construction instructions.)

Arena: An arena should be a minimum of 66 feet by 132 feet, but 100 feet by 200 feet would be better. The fence should be at least 6 feet tall and made from sturdy materials.

34. A safe, strong tie area where a young horse can learn to stand tied, tacked or untacked without pawing, swerving, chewing, or whinnying.

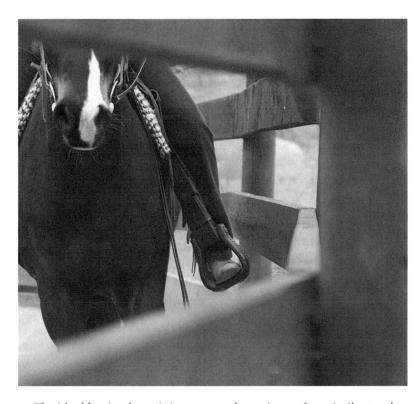

35. The sloped, sturdy walls of this round pen make it ideal for first rides on young horses.

The ideal footing for training a young horse is a surface similar to what he will be worked on as an adult. If a horse is geared for arena competition, a sand round pen and arena with a 4-inch base will be fine for longeing, driving, and riding. Cross-country and endurance prospects would benefit from work on the terrain that will be encountered as an adult; however, working an insecure, unbalanced or unshod young horse in uneven, rocky, or slippery terrain can be dangerous. (See Chapter 6—Riding Out.) Until the youngster gains some experience and conditioning, it is best to hold the training sessions in an enclosed level area that provides adequate cushion.

Safety

Handling young horses can be risky. Because of the nature of the equipment used in restraint and ground training your vulnerability during ground work and first rides and the unpredictable outbursts characteristic of young horses, things can quickly get confusing and dangerous.

By practicing safe horse handling and riding practices you will greatly minimize your chances of accidents when working with a young horse. Most horse-related mishaps are caused by one of the following:

1. A lack of understanding in reading horse body language; lack of experience handling horses; lack of ability not having a way with horses.
2. Carelessness, lack of attention, and over-confidence.
3. Working in unsafe facilities.
4. Inadequate or improper training of the horse.
5. Inadequate or improper training and/or supervision of the handler or rider.
6. Unsuitable horse.
7. Equipment failure.
8. Poor equipment fit.
9. Bad luck such as horse spooks, slips, or falls.
10. Handler or rider hasn't planned for emergencies.
11. Loss of temper.
12. Presence of other horses and riders.

Shortcutting proper safety practices is probably the number one cause of equine-related accidents. Do not attempt to teach a horse something that is beyond your capabilities and do not attempt a maneuver that is far too advanced for a particular horse. Keep the pace of your training schedule conservative and steady.

Commonly, when a horse is faced with a lesson that he is unable to accept or resolve, he reacts with some sort of undesirable avoidance behavior. Rushed training can cause explosive reactions such as bucking, rearing, or running away as well as chronic and sometimes insidious attitudes such as sullenness, uncooperativeness, and boredom.

Because of their size, strength, and quick reflexes, *all* horses are potentially dangerous. A horse's power and unpredictability are often underestimated and can surface unexpectedly, especially when the horse is being presented with something new.

As a safeguard, always carry a sharp pocket knife in case the only way out of a dilemma is to cut ropes. Even though quick release knots and panic snaps are often used, there are times when the weight of a struggling horse can prevent these safety devices from operating.

Because so many ground training procedures involve ropes and long lines, you should become accustomed to wearing gloves for protection against rope burn. Never wrap or loop a rope around your hand, arm, or other part of your body. Wear boots or durable shoes to protect you from the frequent missteps a young horse makes as he gains balance and confidence.

Only use equipment of the strongest type and periodically inspect it for wear so that the young horse will not learn bad habits. Escaping a lesson by breaking a piece of weak equipment can set the stage for a life-long bad habit of attempting to repeat the behavior.

Tack should be well stitched, and constructed from durable materials that are not fatigued from long use, sweat, dirt, sun and/or rain. Hardware should be of the highest quality material and workmanship. Do not use tack that is merely attractive; be sure it will be reliable under severe stress. Make dependability, not cost, your number one priority when choosing training tack.

Review

Before you step up on your horse for the first ride, you should review and re-establish his manners and previous ground training. In-hand work, restraint, longeing, and driving for the yearling and two-year-old were covered in *The Formative Years*. Here I am offering additional and more advanced information on the subjects. Keep a record of the frequency, length, and content of each training session. They will prove valuable when you need to review the horse's progress and will be helpful in designing and modifying your next training program.

Before you start reviewing the specific lessons, think about your overall goals. In general, a riding horse should be trusting, respectful, obedient, relaxed, cooperative, patient, attentive, tractable, and willing (photo 36). How you go about your review work will set the stage for the development of the right mental set. A young horse needs to respect and trust you in order for him to willingly cooperate during his lessons. Reasonable restraint, properly applied, can help you teach your horse respect. Fairness in all of your actions will teach your horse trust.

You must strike a balance between necessary discipline for a horse's mistakes and the preservation of the horse's self-esteem. Some horses, like people, are more fragile and timid than others. Because learning is based on trial and error, if a horse becomes afraid to try anything new because of excessive or unfair punishment, his training will be at a

36. This rider's subjective goals for her two-year-old: an alert, cooperative, and obedient horse. Goals well met.

virtual standstill. On the other hand, some young horses think a little *too* highly of themselves, and in their exuberance to assert their status they can become unmanageable and dangerous.

A few well-planned sessions are more effective than continuous repetition that can make a horse dull or resentful. Lessons that are clear and have appropriate reward tend to encourage a good attitude. Alternating between formal lessons and purely enjoyable human inter-actions (from the horse's point of view) will encourage a horse to look forward to his work. Rewards center around physical gratification, such as food, rest, or grooming. Leading a young horse into the barn to be

37. Review hobbling and require that your horse stand perfectly still for increasingly longer periods of time.

fed, allowing a yearling to rest and roll after a longeing session, or giving a horse a good rubdown after a workout all make pleasant associations with training and the handler.

Enhancement of Ground Training

Use what your horse learned in his yearling and two-year-old years as a foundation for his mounted work. Start with something that you and your horse know well, such as catching, haltering, and turning loose and pay attention to every detail and make it the very best you can. Similarly, review restraint (photo 37), in-hand work, (photo 38) longeing and driving, adding new maneuvers and honing old skills.

38. During in-hand work, hold the end of the rope and the whip in your left hand and work in a position next to the horse's shoulder.

IN-HAND CHECKLIST

Can be caught easily
Can be haltered smoothly
Can be turned loose safely
Will walk alongside handler, handler on near side
Will walk alongside handler, handler on far side
Will perform the following maneuvers with handler on
    either side:
    Stop
    Turn left
    Turn right
    Back
    Turn on the forehand to the left
    Turn on the forehand to the right
    Turn on the hindquarters to the left
    Turn on the hindquarters to the right (photo 39)
    Halt on the long line
Can be easily led with the bridle
Can be led with halter or bridle away from other horses
Can be led over obstacles such as:
    Ground poles
    Plywood or platform
    Concrete
    Plastic or tarp
Can be led by obstacles:
    Flag
    Tractor
    Plastic on fence
Can work a gate in-hand

39. Reviewing the turn on the hindquarters in-hand. Note that at the 90 degree point of the turn the horse has to pick up his pivot foot (right hind) and set it down to reposition it.

LONGEING

Use of Side Reins with Longeing
(Photos 40-47 illustrate the attachment of the longe line and side reins.) Side reins help to balance a moving horse from left to right and begin to introduce contact with the bit. Adjustments to side reins should always encourage the horse to make a physical effort to reach for the bit. The side reins should *never* be so short that the horse cannot avoid contact with the bit. Side reins often snap to the bit and are adjustable

40. One way to attach a longe line to a bridle: Run the longe line through one ring of the bit, over the horse's poll, and attach it to the opposite ring.

41. When longeing to the right, the line will be attached to the left ring and come out of the right ring.

42. In lieu of a longeing cavesson, attach longe line to both halter ring and bit ring on the same side. Note the desirable moist mouth on this young horse.

43. A forward-moving three-year-old with a rubber bit (note chewing) and leather reins adjusted very loose.

44. The leather reins half-hitched to the saddle horn.

45. The elastic side reins have been adjusted to encourage this three-year-old to elongate and slight round his topline.

46. These leather reins have been shortened to encourage this horse to elevate his head and begin collecting the lope.

47. These side reins are much, much too short and have caused the horse to come severely behind the bit. He has lost his forward momentum and his movement has become very stilted.

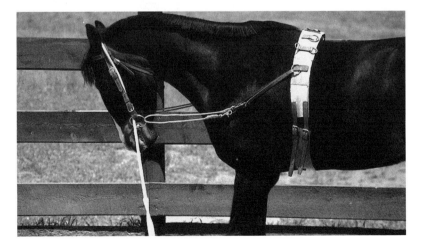

48. Side reins constructed of weak elastic may encourage a horse to root into the bit and play with the reins.

on the other end by means of a leather strap and buckle. Some side reins have a rubber donut incorporated in them. This is thought to offer some degree of flexibility for the horse's jaw and poll, yet if you have ever pulled on one of those rubber donuts you know that it takes a tremendous force to stretch the "elastic" portion of the rein at all, so the yielding benefit is minimal. However, using side reins with very loose elastic inserts or very stretchable bunji cord might encourage a horse to play around with the reins and might cause the development of a persistent habit of head tossing or diving into the bit (photo 48). Using nonelastic reins properly seems to offer no problems.

Benefits of Using Side Reins

* Make the horse focus ahead where he is going, not to one side or the other.
* Minimize the horse's ability to move his head left or right and can limit to some extent his ability to move his head up and down.
* Allow the trainer to introduce light contact to the horse and to progressively add more contact as the horse develops.
* Encourage a horse to reach forward and down for the bit because the back is unburdened by a rider's weight.
* Encourage a horse to develop balance and self-carriage as the reins *gradually* compact his frame.

At first the young horse is allowed to carry very long side reins which let him fall low in front. Although this does let a horse's weight fall on his forehand which is not desirable, it does allow the horse to stretch his back and bring it up. Gradually, with the use of the side reins, the horse's front end is brought up.

The young horse often starts out carrying his nose 20 degrees or more in front of the vertical and throughout all of his first year of work should be allowed to carry his nose at least 10 degrees in front of the vertical so that he can balance himself. The head and neck are the balancing arm of the hindquarters. As the horse gets stronger in the loin and croup, he will be able to carry more weight with the hindquarters and consequently elevate his head and flex more at the poll. At the end of several months in training, some horses willingly carry themselves with the face line 10 to 5 degrees in front of the vertical, but this is the absolute maximum degree of vertical flexion that should be required of a young, developing horse. If a horse is asked to work at or near the vertical prematurely, it may result in a false headset without the much more important aspect of forward movement from the hindquarters.

A horse can tolerate shorter side reins when working at a trot and canter than when working at a walk. The trot and canter both have moments of suspension that allow the horse to regularly round up his topline, which interestingly lengthens the distance along the top of the spine from the poll to the tail but actually shortens the distance from the hock to the mouth, if you will. This means the "frame" is compacted but the topline is elongated which is the ultimate goal of the horse's development—collection.

Side reins should never be used excessively tight to fight a horse or to master it by cruel submission. Shortening of side reins may span three months or more, only shortening them 1/2 inch per week. A trainer must also be careful about how long to work a horse with a newly shortened length of rein. While you are riding you will *feel* when it is time to give your horse a break from the constraints of the new degree of connection, but when you are longeing you may easily miss the visual signs of fatigue. Therefore, only work a horse for a few minutes at a shortened rein intensity before offering him the opportunity to stretch his neck and back. Then resume the new contact. Always end the session with a stretch break.

Adjustment of the Inside and Outside Reins

Assuming the side reins are equal in length (that is, one has not been stretched or broken so that it is a different length than the other) and the adjustment holes are in exactly the same place, the inside rein is generally fastened from one to three holes shorter than the outside rein. This is to allow the horse to gently bend into the direction of the circle and will also cause the horse to take contact with the outside rein. Such an adjustment will help a horse find his balance. Every time a horse moves with an irregular or quick rhythm he is telling you he has momentarily lost his balance and is scurrying to find it.

The outside rein is a stabilizing force which keeps the outside shoulder from pushing out of the circle. A horse worked with a too-tight inside rein and a too-loose outside rein will likely over-bend to the inside and consequently bulge his outside shoulder away from the circle. An increased outside rein contact will help to keep the outside shoulder up under the horse. If a horse is very stiff to the left, for example, he may pull against the left rein and bend to the right, even if he is being worked on a circle to the left. This counter-flexing often results in a concave right side. In a situation like this, at first the outside rein may have to be loosened, the inside rein tightened even more. If the horse is very inexperienced in side reins, rather than tightening the inside rein, you can use repeated tugs with the longe line to bend the horse left.

If a horse falls to the inside, loosen the inside rein and tighten the outside rein to hold him up on the perimeter of the circle. Holding longeing lessons in a round pen is a great way to contain the horse's body and help prevent leaning, stiffening, and counter-flexing without over-using contact with side reins.

As you work your horse on the longe line, aim to develop his gaits so that they are pure and unhurried but with plenty of energy from the hind-quarters. If you allow a horse to rush or work with an uneven or impure rhythm, it will carry over to his saddle work. Influencing the tempo of a horse's gaits on the longe line is one of the most difficult aspects of longeing. You must encourage energy and action from the horse using your body language and the whip while at the same time containing it with the action of your body and the longe line.

49. The spiral at the canter or lope develops balance and introduces collection. Use a 33-foot longe line and allow the horse to canter twice around the 66-foot round pen to establish his rhythm.

50. The line is shortened to 20-25 feet for a 40-50 foot circle. The horse is cantered twice around making sure he is moving forward with energy because he will need it in order to balance into the smaller circle which is coming.

51. The line is shortened to 15 feet for a 30-foot circle. He is cantered twice around in this demandingly small circle. Note how he has to drive up underneath himself and elevate his head to stay balanced. Then, the longe line is gradually lengthened so that he returns to the middle-sized circle for two laps and finally the large circle.

LONGEING MANEUVERS

Teach these to the horse in this approximate order:
Whoa on long line
Walk
Walk to halt transition
Walk to trot (or jog) transition
Working (energetic) trot
Jog
Trot to walk transition
Trot to canter transition
Working (energetic) canter
Lope
Canter to trot transition
Lengthened trot
Spiral in and out at trot or jog
Spiral in and out at regular canter (photos 49, 50, and 51)
Canter to walk transition
Walk to canter transition
Reverse toward trainer

GROUND DRIVING

Ground driving (illustrated in photos 52 through 58) provides added benefits to longeing and should be a part of every trainer's repertoire. While longeing introduces the horse to *contact* with the bit, driving introduces *action* of the bit. For the first time, the horse will feel the movement of your hands on his mouth. Driving lines give you a powerful amount of leverage, so be very careful with your hands. Driving will allow you to improve and add to the maneuvers the horse learned in longeing. Specifically, driving is well designed to teach halting, backing, turning, performing a figure eight, and can be used for very advanced maneuvers for the well-trained horse. Unlike your static position when longeing, when driving you will need to actively move about the driving pen as you work on the various maneuvers.

52. For maneuvers such as halt and back, drive the horse in front of you.

53. For work at the walk and trot, work the horse around you. Here the lines run from the bit through the stirrups of the western saddle which results in a low head carriage. The outside line runs around the hindquarters and allows the trainer to begin balancing the horse laterally.

54. The Danish method of driving utilizes a training surcingle with the lines running through the top terrets. The outside line comes across the horse's back directly to the trainer's hand.

55. Using a surcingle with top terrets encourages a higher head carriage. The trainer stands off to the side of the horse; this is ideal for teaching turning and the figure eight.

56. A steady but light feel on the driving lines is desirable just as in riding.

57. When turning a horse such as in the figure eight, instead of pulling back on the line of the new direction, lift it while allowing the other line to slip gradually through your hand as the horse turns.

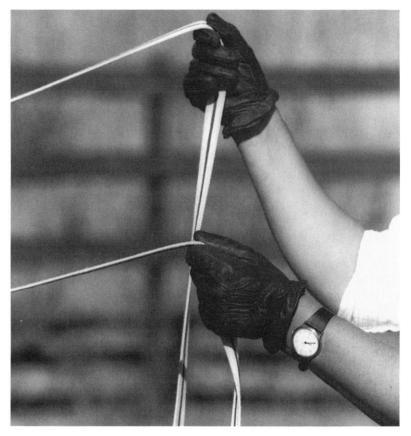

Advanced Driving Lessons

You can use driving lines to introduce your horse to backing as long as you do not overdo it. Standing a safe distance behind your horse in a "plow-driving" position, hold the lines evenly in your hands. Then, with the voice command you used with in-hand work ("BAAAAACK"), gently pull one rein and then the other. Since the back is a two-beat diagonal gait in reverse, using one rein and then the other will more effectively untrack one diagonal pair of legs at a time. Pulling straight back on both reins simultaneously usually results in resistance and no backward movement. At first, be satisfied with a shifting of body weight rearward, releasing after every such response. Eventually, the horse will respond by taking a few steps back (photo 58).

The figure eight is a valuable exercise for introducing turning and the change of rein. Remember that when you use long lines to turn, as you ask for bending with one line, you have to give with the other to allow the horse to bend. Depending on the sharpness of the turn and the gait

58. Driving is an excellent time to introduce the back. This horse willingly rounds into the contact and moves diagonal pairs of legs backward.

and speed in which the horse is working, the giving can be accomplished by letting the outside line (outside of the turn) slide through your hand or you may just have to reach your arm forward or lift you arm to provide the give. When asking for a figure eight with driving lines, follow the pattern of a lazy X configuration at the center of the figure eight, unlike the perfect circle figure eight you will aim for later in riding. The lazy X configuration will allow you to drive your horse on a diagonal line between the two circles of the figure eight. This will provide ample time for the horse to change his bend. If a horse is circling left, the left line is asking him to bend left and the right line is allowing him to bend left. As he approaches the lazy X, the lines should straighten him out

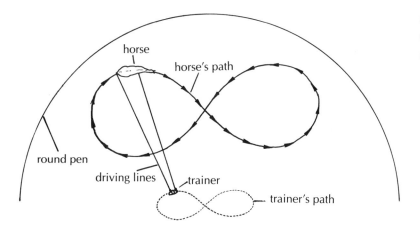

Figure 4. Figure eight for ground driving.

so that when he crosses the center point he is tracking straight ahead, even on both lines. Then the right line asks for a bend to the right and the left line allows it. If in either direction the horse falls onto the inside shoulder, making the circle on that side of the figure eight too small, you will have to hold a little more pressure with your outside line to keep the horse up on his outside shoulder. Most horses will try this on one side of the figure eight and not on the other. This is due to the natural tendency of horses to be one-sided. Figure 4 shows the paths taken by trainer and horse in completing a figure eight.

5

Forward, Straight, and Steady

The Early Mounted Work

Formulating Your Plan

You have a variety of subjective and objective goals to accomplish during your horse's early saddle training. Your long-term goals will vary depending on whether you are training a reining horse or a dressage prospect, a pleasure horse or an endurance horse, a jumper or a roping horse. If you are training a horse for a novice trail rider, safety and comfort of gaits will be of utmost concern. If you are training a dressage prospect, active, forward movement with an emphasis on the enhancement of the gaits will be foremost on your mind. No matter what the horse's eventual role certain universal objectives must be met. Some objectives common to all forms of riding are safe mounting and dismounting, upward and downward transitions, work at all gaits in a straight line and with turning, halting, elementary lateral work, and backing. The work should be approached so that the horse develops a confident, steady manner with a cooperative attitude and free, supple, forward movement characterized by a consistent rhythm. During the lessons, he should accept the bit, respond to the aids, work relatively straight and show the very beginning stages of "speed control": extending (moving on) and collecting (shortening).

This initial training period can be scheduled in several ways. It can take place as a continuous program from spring through fall. Or the very beginning lessons, such as mounting, walking, trotting, and simple turning, can take place during a thirty-day period. Then the horse can be turned out for a few months or an entire winter, and when returned to work, the balance of the early training can take place. It will take from three to twelve months to accomplish the goals outlined in this book. Each horse will respond in his own time frame according to his ability and the ability of his trainer.

The overall goal is to have your young horse do *what* you want him to do *where* you want him to do it and *when* you want him to do it. Of course, your requests must be fair and reasonable at all times. If you make it easy for your horse to do the right thing, he will develop a positive attitude toward his work. If you set things up so that it is physically or mentally difficult for him to do the right thing, he may not look forward to his work. This does not mean that you shouldn't challenge your horse. By all means, he needs to be challenged in order to learn, but present him with requests that he can fill.

Often what a trainer asks of a young horse is the very opposite of what the horse would choose to do on his own. A young horse is frequently unfit, unbalanced, and emotionally unstable. This causes him to travel heavy on the forehand, crooked, and in a haphazard and erratic fashion. We aim to develop steadiness in a young horse. First we teach him what he should and should not do, and then we gradually improve his form in these maneuvers. When we define *how* a horse does what we want him to do we are talking about the *quality* of his actions. To give you the best chance for a comfortable ride and a solid base for more advanced work, your young horse should work in harmony with you, freely going forward with interest and energy in a rhythmic, balanced fashion.

When applied to horses, the word *free* can create confusion in some people's minds. Freedom indicates a lack of restriction and usually brings to mind a horse galloping through a field. Yet free is not necessarily synonymous with wild. A well-trained and disciplined horse can and should move freely. When using free to describe a horse being ridden, it refers to riding him with effective aids that aren't forceful or physically inhibiting. The freely moving horse shows expression in his face, body carriage, and the way in which he lifts his legs, moves his shoulders, and uses his back. To be able to ride a horse freely, yet totally under control is the ultimate goal of riding, which can be achieved in varying degrees by all dedicated riders. To allow a horse freedom, the aids must be applied with correct timing, position, and intensity. It takes years for a rider to refine the means to influence a horse without restricting or blocking the energy from flowing around the horse's body.

There must be harmony between a trainer and a horse so that there is always an open line of communication. To achieve harmony, on some days you may need to acknowledge your state of mind and admit when a change in your attitude might have to take place in order to have a productive training session. Harmony is evident in the expression and carriage of both the horse and rider as they work. Poise, confidence, and interest in work are characteristics of horse and rider harmony. If a rider is tense, out of tune, or in a negative state of mind, the horse's performance will be blocked in some way. A trainer and horse working in harmony are in a state of energized, yet relaxed concentration and make the things they are doing together look smooth and effortless.

Guidelines for a Training Session

The goal of horse training is to bend the horse rather than break him. The art of horse training presents the horse with progressive, well-planned lessons that will alter his behavior in subtle ways.

Horses are much more secure if their role is made perfectly clear. When planning a training session, it is best to have a very specific order of events in mind. Although it helps to be flexible within the pre-established plan, each training session should have a realistic goal.

Distractions prevent the horse in training from giving his full attention to the lesson. For example, it is best to eliminate dogs from the training area, ask that lawn mowing be postponed, and reschedule the turn-out of rambunctious weanlings in the adjacent pasture if you plan to work with a horse that is very young or inexperienced. Eventually, of course, the horse should perform regardless of external conditions, but initially the young horse needs to concentrate without distraction.

One trainer for one horse reduces the chance for confusion from conflicting or even slightly different signals. Once the horse has become steady in his responses, it is wise to begin exposing him to several other competent handlers so that he develops a tolerance for variance.

It is counterproductive to rush during a training session. You need to take whatever time is necessary to move through the progressive steps of a maneuver. Teaching the horse one thing at a time is only logical and fair. Your movements around horses should be smooth but not necessarily slow.

Expect the best from each training session, but be prepared to deal with the worst. With a positive attitude, approach the training arena with the appropriate equipment and safety principles in mind. Play out the "worst case scenario" in your mind ahead of time to help you plan what to do if things do go wrong. Then visualize everything going perfectly.

A typical riding session includes preparation of the horse, warm-up of horse and rider, the training session, warm-down, and post-ride care of the horse. General instructions for every ride on a horse in training follow. Specific recommendations of what to cover each week and month during training will subsequently follow this section.

PREPARATION OF THE HORSE

Your relationship with your horse begins with the first step you take toward him to catch him. As you lead your horse to the grooming area, stay in proper position in the vicinity of the horse's shoulder and be direct and precise in your body language.

Tie the horse or attach him to cross-ties in a manner so that he is safe for you to work on while you are grooming and tacking him. If it is fly season, you may need to begin with a light spray of the legs with a fly repellant. This will make it safer for you to work around his legs.

Put on a pair of barn gloves and begin by picking out the hooves. Grooming continues with loosening dirt, shedding hair, and dead skin and scurf from the horse's skin with a rubber curry on all of the muscled portions. Use a soft rubber grooming tool or mitt to perform a similar function on the horse's head and legs. Then, with a stiff bristled brush whisk the loosened debris from the body with a flicking motion of your wrist. (At this stage of grooming, long sweeping brush strokes would only serve to relocate the dirt.) Use a brush of medium to soft stiffness on the head and legs. Once the majority of the dirt is removed, use a soft brush to finish the coat with long, smooth strokes. Set the coat and remove final dust with a cloth, either dry or damp. Place the saddle blanket or pad on the horse's back slightly ahead of where it will eventually set, then slide it into position. Place the saddle on the blanket, peak the blanket in the gullet of the saddle, and secure the girth or cinch.

In order to keep control of the horse while bridling, untie the lead rope, remove the halter from the horse's head, refasten it around the horse's neck, drape the lead rope over your left arm and proceed to bridle (photo 59).

Hold the bridle in your left hand with the reins draped over your left arm. Reach your right arm over the horse's neck to the off side and bring your right hand near his right ear. Transfer the headstall of the bridle from your left hand to your right hand and then place your left hand on the bridge of the horse's nose. Move your right arm over the top of the horse's neck so your forearm reaches between the horse's ears. This brings the headstall in front of the horse's face. Take the bit in your left hand. Move the bit into position between the upper and lower incisors, then ask the horse to open its mouth by placing your left thumb in the space between the incisors and molars. Once the bit is in his mouth, put

59. Holding the bridle in your right hand between the horse's ears, use your left hand to position the bit near the incisors.

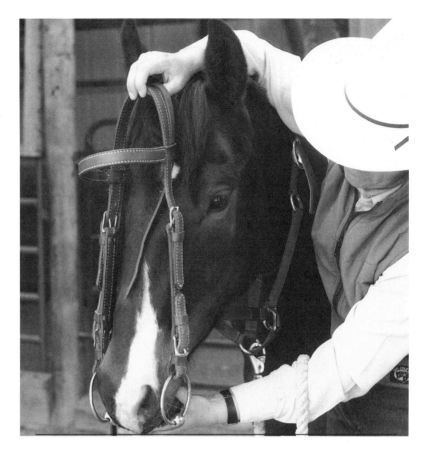

the right ear in the headstall, then the left ear. Check to be sure the bit is centered in the horse's mouth and that the headstall sits symmetrically on the horse's head. Buckle the throatlatch (and noseband if an English bridle). Remove the halter from the horse's neck and you are ready to lead your horse to the arena.

WARM-UP OF HORSE AND RIDER

Leading to arena. Leading a bridled horse is somewhat different than leading a haltered horse. With a lead rope you have one rope that is attached to a ring under the jaw of the horse and you direct the horse with left, right, and backward movements of the rope. A bridled horse has a rein attached to each side of the bit, so if you grab onto the reins together and treat them like a single lead rope, you give confusing and contradictory signals to the horse's mouth. So, separate the reins with your index finger and use the reins independently to indicate to your horse whether he should turn right or left or slow down (photos 60 and 61).

60. When leading with the reins, treat them independently.

61. This young gelding is being warmed up and familiarized with the arena before his first ride there.

When you reach the arena, stop your horse straight and square and give him the command to stand. Routinely take your time preparing to mount, as it will develop patience in your horse. You will need to let down your stirrup irons if you are riding English. Check to see that your saddle is straight, then step in front of your horse and see if your stirrups are even. Give the cinch or girth its final tightening. Put on your gloves, sunglasses, secure your hat, and mount. Sit for just a moment without doing a thing. When *you* decide it is time to move off, give your horse the appropriate signals.

A warm-up decreases the chance of tissue damage from sudden, unusual stresses. It readies the neurological pathways, alerting them for signals, thereby increasing coordination during the more demanding work which will follow. A warm-up increases the blood flow to the skeletal muscles, which increases their strength of contraction and allows muscles to stretch without damage. However, stretching exercises should not be used as the first part of a warm-up as they may result in torn fibers. It is most beneficial to move the horse at a walk for at least 2 to 3 minutes before starting a trot.

A warm-up should consist mainly of an energetic trot at a slow rhythm, not explosive or configurationally demanding work. You will know that your horse is warmed up when he blows (exhales through his nose), breathes long and deep, when he mouths the bit, and begins lowering his head, reaching forward. Almost any horse improves after a warm-up. The lazy horse's blood gets flowing, and he becomes more physically stimulated to work. The hyperactive, hot horse gets the edges smoothed off his neuromuscular signals, which results in smoother, more controlled movements.

THE TRAINING SESSION

If you need help setting goals for a session, start by thinking of the session as several short portions of time rather than one long block of time. Using an hour for an example, if you schedule 10 minutes for a warm-up and plan to save 10 minutes for a warm-down, you have 40 minutes left for the work. You could apportion the 40 minutes this way: review work 10 minutes; break 2 minutes; new work 15 minutes; break 3 minutes; review work 10 minutes and then time for the warm-down. As a horse becomes better trained and conditioned, the break times become shorter and less noticeably different from the work itself.

Depending on a horse's level of training, work him through the following types of work in the order listed.

Forward Work: energetic walk and long trot on straight lines with minimal contact and minimal bending (see photo 62). This is the work for a warm-up and warm-down and in the very early stages of training can be the sole work for both the review session and new work.

Gymnastics: forward work with bending such as large circles, half-turns (reverses), serpentines, change of rein across a diagonal. This work is appropriate for the last part of the warm-up, the review periods, and the new work.

Lateral Work: work involving sideways movement such as turn on the forehand and leg-yielding. This work is appropriate for the new work period.

Connected Work: this the pre-collection work for the young horse involving longitudinal flexion such as walk-trot, trot-walk, trot-canter, canter-trot transitions, and backing. Generally this work should be covered during the new work period and be interspersed with gymnastics and lateral work.

At first, you may find it best to use a watch to keep track of the time as you work. Later you will learn to read your horse's signs and know when it is time to move on to the next segment of the session. Every horse has a different peak period capacity that will increase as his condition improves. Know how long your horse's peak will last and

62. Forward work should be character-ized by a long frame and forward reach. This fresh young horse, although on a loose rein, is working with a short stride and more joint flexion than desirable. He should either be given more time to relax at the walk or be ridden forward actively at the long trot to encourage him to stretch.

63. When it is time
for a break, do not
dump the horse on
his forehand by
letting go of the reins
suddenly. Instead let
him gradually stretch
down into a light
contact.

only work to that point. If you insist that he work past his peak, you risk destroying what you have gained in the previous work. And do not use up all of your horse's energy in the warm-up—be sure to save some energy for the new work.

When you are ready to begin the review portion of the lesson, choose something your horse knows well and is capable of performing with relative ease. It may be circles or serpentines at the walk or quiet trot. It should be active, forward work where you are riding the horse on straight lines, that is, with no lateral work.

When you take the rest break, take care not to "throw the horse away" all of a sudden. A sudden release of the reins will just dump the horse on his forehand. Let him, instead, gradually stretch down. If a horse stretches down, it indicates the review work was successful (photo 63). Feed the reins out to him slowly until he is just moseying around the arena, blowing through his nose. As the rest period comes to a close, drive him forward with your lower legs, slowly pick the reins up again, gradually adding more contact until you have him working in the state he was before the break.

The new work period should include more difficult work such as a series of transitions, lateral work, or introducing something new such as backing or loping small circles. I have shown this in photo 64.

How do you know when it is time to quit the new work? That is an art and science in itself. Although you would like to make a break-

64. During the new work period, introduce new maneuvers or concepts. Here the horse is being asked to begin shifting his balance rearward during a forward lope on light contact.

through during every session, that is not a realistic expectation. Sometimes you need to quit while you are ahead. If a horse has given an honest effort but begins to tire and make mistakes, it is time to move out of the new work period and into the final review or even directly to the warm-down. On the other hand, if a horse is being belligerent and refuses to listen, then you may need to ride him through the difficulty. Rather than fight, walk on a long rein for a moment, rearrange your thoughts, and then return to the work. Once your horse is in good physical condition and you know his level of mental concentration, you may recognize certain days that things are going so well that you can ask for more complex things. When introducing new things, however, there is always the potential of running into a problem. You will have to decide whether you need to resolve a problem or come to a tactful end to the session and deal with the problem during the next ride.

The break after the new work can be a little bit longer than the previous break, but it is similar in format. Remember, a horse's desire to stretch is a result of well-done connected work. Once you have picked your horse back up, you will begin the final work session.

During the closing review period, it is best to identify the areas where the horse may have had problems with the new work so you can go back to the basics that underlie them. Do not work on the new concept itself, but review and reestablish the pertinent foundation principles so that during the next training session, the horse will have a better chance of performing the new work correctly. To preserve a horse's interest in his work, end with something he does well. It is good for you to end with a good opinion of yourself and your training also.

THE WARM-DOWN

After a vigorous ride, it is important to gradually and systematically wind down from the work. Budget 10 to 15 minutes to accomplish this. The warm-down begins when you have given the horse some slack in the reins after the last work period in the session and ends when you have returned to the barn to untack.

The warm-down does not have to consist entirely of walking around on a long rein. It can, and should for very fit horses, include some time trotting freely on a long rein. That sort of loose, relaxed trotting will help flush accumulated lactic acid from the dense muscles of the hindquarters. After a particularly vigorous ride, you may choose to get off, loosen the girth or cinch, and lead your horse for the last 5 minutes either around the arena or down the road.

If your horse is very hot, do not let him cool out too quickly. Keep his back and loin covered with a quarter sheet or wool cooler as his muscles dissipate their heat via evaporation. Spraying a hot horse with cold water will cause his muscles to get stiff. Using water to hose sweat and dirt off your horse every day is not a good long-term management practice anyway. It can result in more problems than benefits. A daily wet/dry situation can be extremely damaging to the structure of your horse's hooves. Horses' hooves are healthiest when they are regularly exercised but kept at a relatively constant dry external moisture level. Also, fungus and skin problems can occur when horses are frequently wetted down and aren't allowed to thoroughly dry.

One solution to cleaning a sweaty horse without hosing him down is to use a body wipe in specific areas such as the head (see photo 65), saddle area, the underside of the neck, and between the hind legs. Body braces are available commercially or you can make your own by filling a gallon plastic milk container with water, adding 2 tablespoons of Calgon water softener, 2 tablespoons of baby oil, and 1 ounce of your favorite liniment. This mixture lifts dirt and sweat off the horse's hair, conditions it, and stimulates the skin. If your horse is very sensitive, you may need to decrease or eliminate the liniment from the formula. With any horse, do not use a body wipe with liniment near the eyes, nostrils or on the anus.

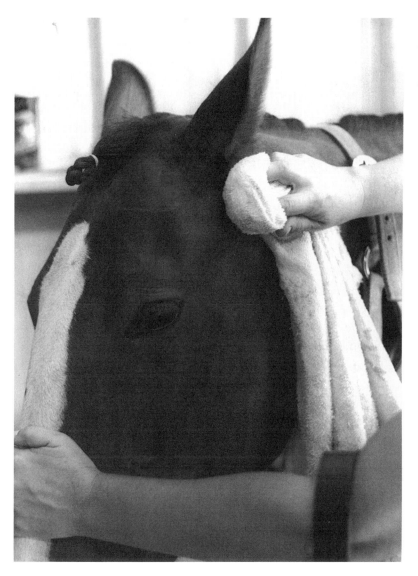

65. After a work-out, an alternative to hosing is to wipe the sweaty areas with a body wash.

After wiping your horse down, leave him tied so he can dry while you attend to your tack. Wipe the mouthpiece and rings of the bit with a damp cloth. Clean the leather portions of your tack with a liquid soap. (Fill a spray bottle with one part Murphys liquid soap to two parts water and use this for everyday cleaning. Use paste, bar, or gel saddle soap for weekly cleaning.) Be careful not to spray the bit with the soapy solution. Wipe all of the sweat and dirt from your tack each time you use it to prolong its life and prevent breakage.

After a sweaty workout, there is nothing a horse likes better than to roll in some soft dirt. Of course a dirty coat will create problems for you the next time you want to ride, so the best bet is to allow the horse to roll in a sandy pen or an arena with sawdust or shavings. After he has had a chance to satisfy his act of self-grooming, brush him or vacuum him, cover him with a sheet, and return him to his stall or pen.

APPROXIMATE ORDER OF THE LESSONS

Mount
Walk
Halt
Turn both ways using leading rein
Dismount
Trot (walk to trot; trot to walk)
Riding corners and large circles
Turn on the forehand both ways
Serpentine, half-turns
Leg-yield both ways
Canter (trot to canter, canter to trot), both leads
Connection
Introduction of the outside aids
Half halts
Square halts
Relative straightness
Backing
Lengthening and energizing gaits
Shortening and slowing gaits
Walk around turn on the hindquarters
Neck reining
Riding with other horses
Riding out
Obstacles

The Training Program

One of the most common questions a developing horse trainer asks herself is, "What should I work on next?" Prioritizing the lessons is important. Although the progression of the lessons is fairly standard, each horse will show you what he needs to learn first and he will also give you signs when he is ready to move on to something.

The actual program will depend somewhat on your long-term goals and the condition of your horse at the beginning of the program. (See Chapter 7 for more information on conditioning.) Assuming the horse has been prepared for saddle training with an appropriate review of ground work and all necessary clipping and grooming, here are approximate guidelines for the actual riding sessions:

First week: first five rides: pre-ride warm-up 15 minutes; ride 5–20 minutes; 2 days off or as needed.

Second week: shorten or eliminate the pre-ride warm-up if possible; ride 15–25 minutes four to five times; 2 to 3 days off as needed.

Third week: pre-ride warm-up optional; ride 30 minutes four to five times; 2 to 3 days off as needed.

Fourth week: eliminate pre-ride warm-up; ride 45–60 minutes; 2 to 3 days off as needed.

Second month: ride 30–60 minutes 3 to 5 times per week.

Third month: ride 30–60 minutes or more 3 to 5 times per week.

Fourth through twelfth month: ride 30–60 minutes or more 3 to 5 times per week.

THE FIRST MONTH

Getting Ready to Mount

As the time approaches for you to mount your young horse for the first time, are you anticipating a fight, an explosive surprise, or do you see things going like clockwork with both you and your horse emerging winners? It is natural to experience anxiety before mounting a horse for his first ride—that is just horse trainer's normal stage fright. A small amount of apprehension will probably make you pay closer attention to safety. Being alert primes your nerves and muscular actions. But *too much* tension can take the smoothness and confidence out of your moves and that might bring undesirable reactions from your horse.

The best way to make the first mounting just another day in the string of lessons for your young horse is to precede mounting with the proper ground training. Contrary to what you might think, the vast majority of accidents with young horses are not due to a horse being sneaky or dishonest and pulling out all the stops on mounting day. Most young horses act very honestly and predictably and are merely reflecting their previous handling. Accidents with young horses can usually be traced to the violation by the trainer of one or more very simple, basic safety rules or to the omission of important basic ground training. Even the most experienced, accomplished trainers consistently emphasize the importance of the basics. So take the previous review work seriously. The true test of when your young horse is ready to mount is whether you can actually *do* the things listed in Chapter 4 with him. Can you?

The overall goal of the first few rides is to reinforce the horse's trust in you. He must overcome his inborn fear of having "an animal" on his back. To further a horse's trust in you, never do anything that will scare or hurt him. You should aim to develop a partnership, one in which you are definitely in charge but not one in which the horse is inhumanely dominated by rough tactics. *Earning a horse's trust and respect simultaneously is the foundation of horse training.* A young horse needs to know in very clear terms that you are the boss and that what you request, he must do. But you want willing compliance, not a broken-spirited submission. What you ask of your horse must be based on sound horse training principles and must be consistent.

THE PRE-MOUNTING WARM-UP

Currently it is not a widespread practice to wear a protective helmet when riding, yet more and more trainers and instructors advise the use of a "hard hat," especially when riding young horses. Boots with heels are an important safeguard because certain stirrups can allow a nonheeled boot or shoe to slip through them and trap the rider's foot. If gloves are used, they should be of the type that allow grip and a feel of the reins. A thick or heavy pair of gloves can make for cumbersome movements.

You can use in-hand work, longeing, driving, or ponying to take the edge off a young horse prior to his first ride. Whatever method of warm-up you choose, it should be very familiar to the young horse. It would make no sense to introduce a new ground training lesson on the day of your first ride.

You can choose to take your first rides using a halter and lead rope, bosal, or snaffle bridle. It is not so important *what* you use on his head, but *how* you use your body. Although it is good to keep your mind open to different methods for the future, for the moment choose the method with which you are most comfortable and proficient. The pre-ride warm-up and the first ride should take place in a safe enclosed area. I prefer a 66-foot diameter round pen with sturdy walls and sand footing.

Begin the session as if nothing out of the ordinary is planned. Be sure you do not have time constraints because if you are in a hurry, it will surely affect your work. Be thorough with haltering, leading, tacking up, and leading to the round pen. Warm your horse up by leading him in-hand for a few moments to "untrack" him. Check the cinch for appropriate tightness and then ready the horse for longeing, driving, or ponying. The pre-ride warm-up should take the edge off the horse but not tire him out. He will need to be alert and have muscle strength and energy left if you expect him to pay attention and actually learn something from the first mounting lesson.

After the warm-up, check the cinches (and breast collar if used) once again and be sure they are snug but not uncomfortably tight. Be sure to remove the stirrup hobble rope if you used one for driving. Square the horse up so he will have an easier time maintaining his balance as you mount. If he has one front foot way out to the right, for example, he will likely bring it under his belly with a quick motion when you begin mounting. If one hind leg is far behind, the horse will probably step forward as you begin mounting. Either of these circumstances may make you think he is going to walk off. This might make you lose your concentration or balance, or you may instinctively snatch at the reins and start a cycle of errors. Any time you have difficulty in the chain of events, and this goes for the horse's entire training, stop, go back to where you and your horse were comfortable and performing well, and proceed from there.

Mounting

Although you have been able to prepare the young horse for almost every sensation he will experience during the first ride, three things that *will* be new to him are the feel of your legs on his sides, the feel of your weight on his back, and the sight of you above and behind him.

I like to start young horses with a western saddle even if they are destined to be used as English horses. First of all, the weight of an empty western saddle does a better job of accustoming a horse's back to carrying. Second, western stirrups and fenders familiarize the young horse with movement against his sides preparing him for the feel of your legs. Third, when properly fitted a western saddle has less of a tendency to shift when a rider mounts. This is due to the friction of the large contact area of the skirts and the wrapping and enveloping effect that a western saddle tends to have. Fourth and perhaps most important a western saddle has a larger bearing surface than an English saddle so it distributes a rider's weight over a larger area of the horse's back muscles. A horse's back is like a suspension bridge, not really well-designed to carry weight. The horse's neck, abdominals, and back muscles already have a big job suspending the weight of his abdomen. Now the muscles must work even harder to keep the back from sagging under the weight of the saddle and rider. The longer, wider bars of a properly fitted western saddle make bearing the weight of the rider more comfortable for the young horse. Once the horse's back has begun to strengthen and develop, it can more easily bear a rider's weight via the panels of a properly fitted English saddle.

To prepare a horse for you being above him during riding, when you groom or clip him, step up on a box or when he is turned out, sit on the top rail of his pen and let him come up and investigate you.

Become aware of your everyday mounting habits (on already trained horses) that could use improvement. Do the toes of your left boot dig into a horse's side as you rise to mount? Pointed toe boots are particularly inappropriate when mounting unless you choose to mount facing forward. Does the saddle shift way off to the left side because you have to pull yourself up with your arms rather than lift yourself up with the muscles of your left leg? Do you wobble as you swing over the horse and throw him off balance or bump him on the croup? Does your seat land with a thud in the saddle or do you have the muscle control to lower yourself softly into the saddle? Does your right leg slap his side as you find your position or do you let your leg settle softly on his side? If you have any of these problems, practice mounting a safe, trained horse until your bad habits are replaced with good ones. Here is one place where being in good physical condition will help you perform more effectively and safely.

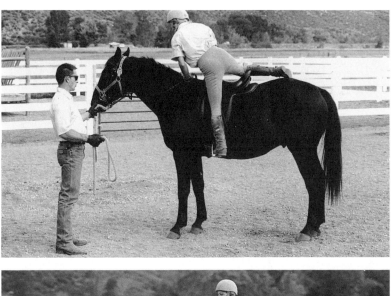

66. For this two-year-old's first mounting, a handler is assisting.

67. The handler leads the horse in a customary fashion while the rider sits quietly with light hands and minimal leg contact.

68. Gradually the handler lets out more lead rope turning over the guiding of the horse to the rider.

69. The handler unsnaps the lead rope but continues to walk beside the horse for a few laps.

70. Relieved that all went well, the rider thanks her horse and handler. However, the loose reins and the vulnerable forward position of the rider are unsafe.

STYLES OF MOUNTING

Over the years, young horses have been safely mounted in a variety of ways. Choose the style of mounting that you can perform most easily and safely. Do not change your style of mounting the day of the first ride because somebody says it is the only way to mount young horses.

You can mount young horses the same way you do experienced horses: Face the opposite direction the horse is facing, put your left foot in the stirrup, bounce on your right leg while rotating on your left foot in the stirrup. Rotate toward the horse, then forward, rising on the

71. Some trainers prefer to take the first ride alongside a pony horse. Here the young horse is warmed up.

72. The trainer has mounted and is being ponied by the steady, older horse. Note the dally of the lead rope around the saddle horn.

second bounce. If you are accustomed to this method, it will work well for you. In the unlikely event that a horse begins to move off, you will tend to be swung up into the saddle as he moves forward. This style of mounting is safe when used following a thorough restraint and ground training program.

Some riders prefer to approach mounting and the first ride with the aid of a handler on the ground with a long lead rope or the help of a rider on a pony horse. (Photos 66, 67, 68, 69, and 70 show a ground person series; photos 71 and 72 a pony horse.) If working with a very sensitive, rather spooky horse you may wish to consider one of these methods. The rider might get a leg up from yet another assistant so that the rider can lie over the horse's back without a foot in the stirrup. The rider then slides down, gets another leg up, and continues until the horse is relaxed enough to allow the rider to swing a leg over and sit up.

Experienced riders who spend less time on ground training or are starting rough or spoiled young horses might prefer to mount facing the same direction as the horse. Place only the toe of your boot in the stirrup so that if the horse takes off, your foot comes out of the stirrup easily. Often the reins or lead rope are held rather snug with the horse's nose tipped to the left. In some cases the rider might even hold onto the sidepiece of a halter that the young horse wears under its bridle. This may give a trainer more control in some situations, but it does tend to throw a horse off balance. With a thorough ground training program, however, you should be able to allow a young horse to stand square and straight when you step up on him for the first time.

THE FIRST MOUNTING

If you are using split reins, tie them together in a knot about 8 inches from where you will hold them. With your horse squared up, tell him "WHOA," then turn to stand alongside his near side. Take the reins and a portion of his mane near the withers in your left hand as shown in photo 73. If you have done a thorough job of restraint, you will not have to use a tight rein to prevent him from moving forward. However, even with a seemingly quiet horse, have some degree of even contact on the reins because if the horse is suddenly startled and darts forward you do not want to have to paw through a lot of leather before you can make contact with his mouth.

With your right hand, present the stirrup to your left foot (photo 74). Place your left foot securely on the tread, keeping the left side of your body and your left knee as close to the horse's body as possible. That way your knee can act as a pivot point as you swing up to mount. This will decrease your tendency to pull the saddle off center (toward you) as you mount. Bouncing two times seems to provide enough momentum so that you can get up quickly without twisting. Another helpful hint is not to grab the horn or cantle to pull yourself up but rather place your right hand on the off swell of the saddle (photos 75 and 76). Push

73. To mount, tie split reins in a knot, stand facing the rear of the horse, grab the mane and the reins with your left hand.

off to the right and downward on the swell as you make your final rise and let your palm swivel as you swing over onto the saddle. This will help keep saddle slippage to a minimum (photos 77 and 78).

If you find the horse skeptical about being mounted, just step up into the stirrup, bounce a few times, take your foot out of the stirrup, and walk to his head and tell him everything is "OK." If you sense that the horse may be touchy about weight on his back, you can step into the left stirrup, rise, and lean over the saddle keeping both legs on the near side. For safety, once you have leaned over the saddle like this, slip your left foot out of the stirrup, so that when you need to you can just slide down.

When you are ready to swing your right leg over, keep your right knee straight so that you don't bump it on the horse's croup or the cantle. Settle your weight into the saddle softly by using your abdominals and the thigh muscles of your left leg to gradually let yourself down. Do not land with a thud or your horse might be off running! And do not grope wildly for the right stirrup with a flailing right leg or lean over to grab

74. Standing as close to the horse as possible, with your right hand turn the left stirrup and present it to your left foot. Place your foot securely on the tread.

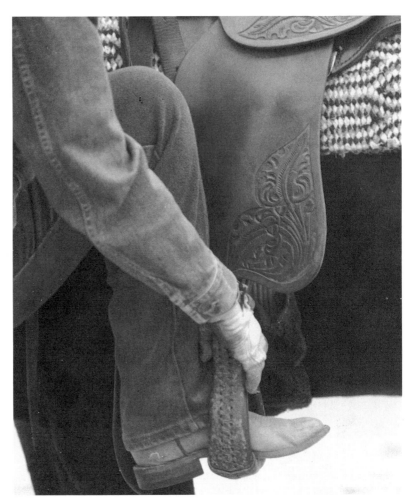

it. I have seen riders' overconcern for finding the right stirrup be the cause of young horses' anxiety. When a horse feels the rider's leg fluttering around looking for the stirrup, he may walk off or spook. Just sit in a balanced position with your legs off the horse's ribs for the time being.

Resist the temptation of leaning forward to pet your horse on the neck as this will put you in a vulnerable, off-balance position. And if the horse is startled by you leaning forward, he may raise his head or neck suddenly and bop you on the nose. If you feel the urge to reassure your horse that all is well, say something in a pleasant tone and give him a scratch on the withers. Use one word or a short phrase. A lot of talking at this time can be confusing, especially if the young horse has been trained to voice commands during ground work. Sit quietly, well-

balanced, and deep in the saddle—the safest position to be in if something exciting does happen. If you are on an especially sensitive horse, you may wish to spend the majority of the first lesson mounting and dismounting. Or you may want to work the horse a little and then practice the mounting and dismounting at the end of the lesson.

In either event, eventually you have to take your right stirrup. Repeat the command "WHOA" as you carefully hook the off stirrup with the toe of your boot. If at any time your horse reacts to your movements by walking off, use your voice command "WHOA" with a very light lifting of the reins.

The First Ride

After you have been mounted for 5 to 15 seconds or so, it is time to move off. There is no hurry and it is best to sit for an increasingly longer spell *every* time you mount. Use a voice command (such as "Walk on") or the clucking noise that you used in longeing to get your horse moving. Add a light squeeze with both legs.

75. (above left) Keeping your knee close to the horse's side to act as a pivot point, place your right hand on the off swell and push down on the swells as you begin your upward rise.

76. (above right) Sit still for a moment before you rebalance the saddle if necessary and before you ask the horse to move off.

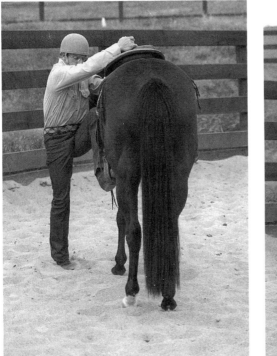 

77. (above left) If you grab the saddle horn or the cantle with your right hand,

78. (above right) you will tend to pull the saddle off to the left as you rise.

If your young horse is confused and stays rooted, take one rein out to the side to cause him to shift his balance sideways. Using a leading or opening rein will cause him to step toward that rein. As soon as he moves the first leg, return the rein to its "neutral" position near the saddle horn as you cluck again and give a gentle squeeze. Most frequently if a horse is properly prepared, he will allow you to mount up and walk off as if there is very little new in the lessons that day.

Now that you are safely in the saddle, you have a most exciting opportunity underneath you. A young horse is like a fresh piece of clay that you can mold and shape to become your fluid, light, and responsive partner. From the beginning, keep him relaxed, attentive, willing, and respectful and you will enjoy many rides to come.

THE LEGS MEAN GO, THE SEAT MEANS SLOW

The first ride can last a few minutes or as long as 20 minutes. If all is going well, aim for at least 10 minutes of mounted time because it will give the horse a chance to relax. If you get on a tense horse and walk around for a minute and get off, you haven't accomplished more than

79. With a relatively light contact on the reins, this rider has squeezed with both legs and asked the horse to stretch into a light contact and walk.

mounting. Perhaps that was your main goal. But you should be able to at least walk and halt during the first ride.

You must teach the horse that when he feels both of your lower legs squeeze his sides in the middle position (on or slightly behind the girth), that means to move forward. With relatively light contact on the reins squeeze with both legs (photo 79). Add a cluck or voice command if necessary. If he's frozen to the spot, untrack him by using a leading rein and giving with the other rein.

If your horse trots or canters, don't make a big deal out of it. Follow him around until you feel him relax and then still the motion of your seat and sit deep, to encourage him to settle his weight to the rear. This should slow him down or even make him stop.

When you first ask a young horse to halt, do not expect to get promptness or squareness. Your goal at first is a smooth forward stop without resistance and with a minimal use of the reins. Your main aid for a stop is your seat. When the horse is walking, follow the action of the hind legs with your seat. Then stop following the motion—make your seat still by flexing your abdominals. (Take care that you do not inadvertently squeeze the horse with your lower legs too much at this stage.) Often, stilling the following motion of your seat, by itself, will cause the horse to slow down or stop. If necessary, add the voice command "whoa" in a long, soothing tone of voice. In some cases, and certainly later on in the horse's training, you will need to add a very light and smooth but firm gathering of the reins to further cause the weight to be shifted to the hindquarters. However, never pull back roughly on the reins; this will scare the horse, cause him to tense his neck and back, and lock you out. Inappropriate pressure in a horse's early training can make a life-long association with resistance to rein aids. Think of stopping your horse using 90 percent weight, seat, and upper body and 10 percent reins. If you start light you have a better chance of keeping the horse light once you start adding pressure.

Once your horse is stopped, you will want him to stand still for general principles and so that you can dismount. Often young horses find it difficult to stand still under a rider's weight, especially after a work session that has caused his back to become tired. A young horse may move around in an attempt to find a comfortable way of supporting the rider's weight. If you are sitting unbalanced coming into a stop, then the horse will likely stop crooked with his legs spread out and may shift around looking for a composite balance. Often a rider, out of habit, will shift a slipped saddle back to one side or the other immediately after stopping and this also could cause a young horse to move around. So be careful with these early stops. Always stop on a straight line, not a curve. Approach the stops in a balanced manner, sit quietly once stopped, and gradually build up the amount of time you require the horse to stand still under you. Practice making the horse stand still at the beginning of the lessons as well as at the end. Later on, as the horse develops his strength and balance, you can work on stopping him square and making him stand for extended periods of time.

DISMOUNTING

Be sure the horse is relatively square when you start your dismount so that he doesn't move to balance himself just as you are swinging off. Move your left stirrup tread from the ball to the toe of your boot so that you can get rid of the stirrup quickly if necessary. Then remove your right foot from the stirrup. Put your right hand on the off swell. Say "whoa" and begin shifting your weight over to the left side of the horse (photo 80). Keep your right leg straight and swing it smoothly over the

horse's back, keeping your weight centered over the horse (photo 81). Step down close to the horse facing approximately the same way he is facing. Alternatively, you can take both feet out of the stirrups, lean slightly forward as you swing your right leg over, swivel on your crotch and your left hand (which is on the swells or withers), and slide down. Sometimes this latter method startles the horse if you land with a sudden thud. Whichever method you choose, move as smoothly as possible.

Nine times out of ten, if a horse has had proper ground training, the first ride occurs without a hitch. Sometimes, however, a young horse will spook, run, fall, buck, or rear. Usually such problems indicate inadequate preparation. You need to go back, review sacking and longeing with side reins, or driving. If you find yourself in a problem situation and you are a good enough rider, ride out the storm using your good balance to stay with the horse. If you are in a round pen, the horse can't go very far.

Keep the horse from getting his head down as this often leads to bucking. But be careful how abruptly you pull on the reins because it could cause an explosive reaction such as rearing and the horse could lose its balance and fall over backward. If you do get bucked off, you

80. (above left) To dismount, begin shifting your weight over to the left side of the horse.

81. (above right) Stay close to the horse as you swing your right leg over and step down facing the front of the horse.

have two choices. Either get back on right away or have a better rider take over for you.

Don't forget to emphasize forward movement. Do not be in a hurry to get the horse on the aids, or to teach him a long list of specific maneuvers. Instead, encourage him to move forward freely and naturally. Remember all throughout the horse's work *it is not what you do but how well you do it* that is important. If a horse does not learn to move forward, how will you later be able to press him on to get to a cow, go over a jump, turn it on for a rundown, or to extend his trot? Active, forward energy is essential in all gaits and transitions and is one of your first and most important goals.

If you find that your young horse has a great deal of forward motion, that is the horse trots energetically, canters, or even tries to run away, I think you have a diamond in the rough. You have several choices in dealing with excess forward energy. If you are an accomplished rider, you can sit and ride it out, taking care not to pull at the horse's mouth. When you sense the horse is running out of breath, you can start communicating with your seat sit, deep and ask for a walk and go on from there. Or you could return to ground training to relax the horse and better prepare him for riding. Or you could have a qualified professional ride the horse for you until his forward motion is more suitable for your skill level.

But above all, take care not to pull on the reins during the early rides because you may start a life-long dislike in the horse for going forward. Once a horse is reluctant or afraid to move forward, you have a long remedial program ahead of you. It is difficult to ride well if you must continually prod a horse along. A horse that is eager to step forward with his hind legs will be easier to shape into upward and downward transitions as well as turning. Such a horse will feel like he is energetically and willingly stepping up into your light hands.

A horse without sufficient forward energy, on the other hand, has learned to back away from the contact with the bridle and he probably moves with short, tense steps. Or he might move lazily with sloppy leg movements, falling apart in the middle, which might make you feel as if you are riding two separate horses—one in front of you and one behind. The energy that the horse generates with his hindquarters provides you with the means to tie all of your aids together and increases your chances for a unified movement with the horse. So do not discourage it.

Second Ride

In terms of your preparation, approach the second ride as if it was the first. Review everything that was covered in the first ride. You may find trouble spots that didn't surface the first day. Be sure to work on those. Don't get excited and begin to cut corners. *The slower you go, the faster you will get there.* If you take the time to emphasize the basics, you will experience fewer setbacks. As you design the goals for each lesson, use a "result meter" rather than a clock or calendar to tell you when it is time to move on. Aim for thoroughness, not quick results.

If all goes well, you should add the trot during the second ride. Although a posting trot might be easier on a young horse's back, the up-and-down motion, especially the shifting of balance if you are not quite perfect at posting, might startle the horse. Therefore, you might be better off asking for a very quiet trot and sitting the trot.

Squeeze with both legs, following the motion of the horse's back with a lightly rolling pelvis. Be sure you do not try to straighten, shape, or turn the horse. Let him go pretty much where he wants to go. If you are working in a round pen, he will be encouraged to go in a circle (photo 82).

82. The second ride on a two-year-old. Note:
* Ride is taking place in a round pen with sand footing.
* Rider is wearing safety helmet.
* Horse is holding himself in a typical young horse frame as he trots (see Chapter 7).
* Horse's ears are aimed back, tuned to the rider and the new sensation on his back.
* Contact is light and even on the o-ring snaffle.
* Rider carries a whip in the inside hand to use if necessary to keep the horse moving forward.

The trot is the most important gait for early training because most horses perform it in the most balanced and cadenced fashion of all of their gaits. In these early lessons, the trot can be very quiet with only a small degree of energy coming from the hindquarters. Later on, when you get to energetic trot work such as is a part of dressage training, it is good to work not only in large circles but also in large open spaces so that minimal turning is involved. Use the trot to become aware of your horse's natural rhythm; focus on his rhythm at all gaits during all future lessons.

RHYTHM

Rhythm is the steady tempo within each gait. A gait is pure when it conforms to a precise footfall pattern that has a regular metronome-like rhythm to it. Rhythm refers to not only the true two-beat time of the trot, the three-beat time of the canter, and the four-beat time of the walk, but also to the precise landing of pairs of legs within those time signatures (Figure 5). For example, in the trot and canter diagonal pairs of legs are supposed to land together. If they do not, if the front lands first, then the rhythm is impure due to the fact that the horse is on the forehand.

The regularity of a horse's steps is a very important component of riding. Each gait is like a simple musical piece written in its own time. Every horse plays that piece in his own particular tempo and with his own personal expression. Many horses have one or two gaits that do not have an even, precise rhythm. In order to effectively influence and correct an impure rhythm, you must first allow the horse to establish his natural rhythm, even if it is too fast or too slow. Once you are in tune with that rhythm, *and only then,* can you have any hope of adjusting it. It takes a young horse between four and six weeks to find the aids that will allow you to make substantial adjustments in his rhythm. In the meantime, do not hinder the horse's natural rhythm by trying to slow him down, set his head, or straighten his body. I guarantee that if you do these things before establishing rhythm and steadiness you will wish you had not.

It is helpful when you are working on recognizing, establishing, and influencing a horse's rhythm that you train yourself to have a very specific idea in your mind of what rhythm is. You can count out loud or watch a metronome in your mind to monitor rhythm. Music can help you to establish or maintain your sense of inner rhythm and if appropri-

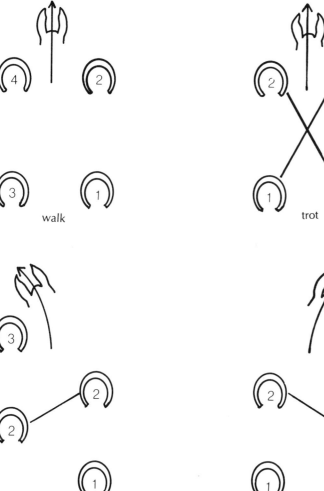
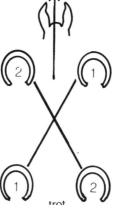

walk

trot

lope (canter) left lead

lope (canter) right lead

Figure 5. The gaits.

ate for a particular gait, can be useful in developing a horse's rhythm as
well. Very small portable electronic metronomes are also available.
Continually refer to your horse's ideal rhythm patterns in your mind as
you work. Otherwise, as your horse speeds up or slows down, he will
tend to make you forget the target rhythm.

A regular rhythm will provide you with a predictable set of movements on which to base the delivery of your aids. When you can depend
on a horse to move his legs in a precise and very even two-beat, three-
beat, or four-beat time, you will find it much easier to stay with the
movement of the horse, find your seat, and stabilize your hands.

Rhythm is inherent to some degree but can be further developed in both the horse and rider through practice.

THE WALK

Properly executed, the walk is a flat-footed, four-beat gait. When performed correctly, it has a very even rhythm between the feet as they land and take off in the following order: left hind, left front, right hind, right front, left hind, and so on. This gives the rider a slightly side to side motion as well as a rear to front motion in the saddle. A horse that can really walk out gives what is called "a rein swinging walk."

If a horse is in a hurry, though, he may have trotting on his mind and may not settle down into an even flat-footed walk. He may seem to be walking on the tiptoes of his hind hooves which may make him jig (a cross between a walk and a trot) or pace (where the distinct four-beat pattern has been rushed and he is using his two right legs together and his two left legs together resulting in a lateral, pacey walk). If a horse is very slow at the walk, you can encourage him to drive off with greater energy with his hind legs. Before you formally try to change how energetically a horse is walking, however, first get in tune with his natural walking rhythm, even if it is too slow.

The Third Ride

The third ride has a reputation among horse trainers for being the time when the horse might ask some interesting questions. To this point the horse has figured out the new sensations involved in being ridden, has regained any confidence that might have been lost by being dominated by a creature on his back, and might be getting a little sore in some places from the new demands on his muscles. The main question horses seem to ask around the third ride is "Do I have to?" It is understandable that they might question this new dimension of work and you must be ready to answer fairly but firmly "Yes." And the best way to do that is with a good measure of forward work at the trot.

TROT

The trot is usually a very regular gait with two distinct beats. It is more stable and precise than the walk or canter. Since the trot is the best gait

83. A two-year-old in a quiet western jog with head carriage, nose position, and rein contact just right for this stage.

of most horses, it is most likely the gait that can help your horse develop his rhythm and balance (note the differences in movement among photos 83 through 87). At the trot, the horse's legs move in diagonal pairs in a metronome-like fashion, clicking off an even one–two rhythm.

The right front and left hind legs rise and fall together, and the left front and right hind legs work together. You can hear, feel, and see this rhythm. Without leaning over, glance at your horse's left shoulder and you will see a distinct change in the muscular shape and configuration of the shoulder as the left front leg reaches out, lands, and flexes. As the front shoulders alternate in their movement, their corresponding diagonal hind legs are also alternating. The term *trot* refers to the gait performed under English tack with a greater length of stride and impulsion than the jog which is the western version of the trot and is shorter strided and usually less energetic. If the diagonal pairs get broken and no longer land at the same time, the horse is performing a four-beat gait instead of a two-beat gait. If jogging excessively slow, the front feet will land before the hinds, causing the horse to be heavy on the forehand, and the horse will appear to be jogging in front and walking behind.

Fourth Ride

From now on, it is up to you to customize your horse's training program. If you pay attention to your horse, he will show signs when he is ready to learn something new. You will also sense when it is time to move from the round pen to the arena to pastures to trails and when it is time

84. A young horse flexing on light rein contact at a quiet jog.

85. The same horse moments later pushed forward into more rein contact resulting in a more active trot with more reach.

86.This three-year-old warmblood strongly reaches forward and his trot is correspondingly long and free.

87. This horse is tense, short strided, and hollow in the back, causing him to trot strung out behind and be above the bit. He needs to be moved more actively forward.

to go back to the round pen or arena for review. I will continue to outline the areas you need to work on in their approximate order, but you will have to determine when to move on, when to shift the order of things, and when to take a break. Be sure to keep all of the overall goals in mind as you add specific maneuvers to your horse's repertoire.

The Balance of the First Month

LISTENING TO THE SEAT

Soon you must make an association with your young horse about the role of your seat. When you still your seat, it means for him to slow down. When you deepen your seat, it should cause him to step more deeply underneath himself with his hind legs and slightly round his back. Begin incorporating a significant number of upward and downward transitions in your sessions. Once a horse is well warmed up, in most cases, it would then do him more good to do ten walk/trot, trot/walk transitions in the next 5 minutes or so than to trot without interruption for 5 minutes. As you walk, press your lower legs on his sides and yield with your hands as he moves forward into trot. Follow his motion with a supple back and a deep but light seat. Then still the following motion of your back and seat until he walks. Repeat this often.

It is the cornerstone of all of the work to come. Transitions are the key to getting your horse on the aids and should be frequently worked into the lessons.

ACCEPTANCE

There is a big distinction between accepting the bit and accepting contact with the bit. In the early lessons, all you expect a young horse to do is to accept the bit; that is, to carry the bridle and bit without demonstrating any undesirable habits such as nose flipping, head shaking, boring down to the ground, rubbing his head, putting his tongue over the bit, and so forth. Later on, you will introduce contact, a light but steady feel between your hands and the horse's lips and mouth. And after that, you will introduce progressively greater degrees of contact in order to produce flexion. But that is a way down the road. For now, be happy if your young horse accepts the bit and bridle. He can hold the bit quietly in his mouth or work it with his tongue, but he should not chew the bit with his teeth. If he does, check bit fit and bridle adjustment or consider using a noseband.

DEVELOPING SUPPLENESS

Suppleness is muscular compliance without tension and stiffness. Suppleness does not indicate slack muscles however, but muscles working with dynamic relaxation, muscles that are working energetically but with flexibility. Signs of suppleness in a horse include a loose, swinging tail that is held up and away from the anus; a horse that moves on a light rein; a horse that will reach down at all gaits; a horse that exhales air through the nostrils by blowing as he works; a horse that is attentive yet has a soft, content, inward focus.

The horse's back is the area where most tension originates and is evident. During training, the back must be systematically strengthened and at the same time relaxed. There are at least two theories regarding how to accomplish this. One states that riding a horse in a long, low frame causes a stretching type elongation of the entire spine which allows the back muscles to raise in a relaxed state and eventually become stronger. The other theory is that riding a horse elevated in front and down in the hindquarters relatively early in the training has the effect of rounding the horse's back (flexing the back muscles) which strengthens and develops the back muscles more effectively while still elongating the entire topline.

The second theory is inappropriate for the first rides on a young horse but holds merit as a goal towards which to work. A blending of the two theories is the key to developing most horses. How much of each theory you incorporate will depend on your abilities as a rider, your eventual goal and use for the horse, and the horse's conformation and natural tendencies. It is best to not use either stretching or rounding to an extreme in the training of any horse, however, as back and leg problems can result from a horse carrying itself in one configuration for an extended period of time. When designing the style of your training, be sure you understand the principles involved and where you are headed; start at a conservative point, make changes gradually, monitor regularly, and make adjustments as necessary.

TURNING

In the early stages, when you reach a corner of the arena, you won't ask the young horse to bend deeply into it. Instead, you will allow the horse to make a gentle turn by using a very light inside leading rein and giving with the outside rein. You will lean your weight slightly to the inside of the turn. Your legs will be relatively passive at this point. Soon, however, you will begin adding your inside leg at the girth to trigger the curling reflex and to give the horse a reference point around which to bend. Your outside leg will continue to be passive for the time being. But for your inside leg to be really effective you must teach your horse the difference between what you want when you use your leg *at* the girth and *behind* the girth. A leg at the girth means move forward. A leg behind the girth means move sideways and forward. Lateral work is coming.

ENERGIZING THE WALK

Sit with a relaxed seat and legs and let your body sway in time to the movement of the horse's back and hind legs. Do you find that in one moment your right leg swings against the horse's barrel while at the same time the left leg swings away from the barrel? And in the next

moment the opposite occurs? Allow yourself to sway side-to-side exaggeratedly. Then, just as your right leg comes in contact with the
horse's right side, press with your right calf, then immediately release
so that you can press with your left calf on the next phase of the sway
of his body.

Continue this encouragement with your lower legs in time with the
horse's rhythm and you will find that he will begin stepping more energetically and with longer strides. Then take a break from this influencing and note that the horse may slow down. Then begin influencing him
again. Do this until you can really feel a difference between the horse
walking at his own rate and the horse walking at a more energetic rate
as influenced by your legs and seat. This is the beginning of your influence over the horse.

THE SECOND AND THIRD MONTHS
Introduction of the Leg for Lateral Movement

Lateral movements are those maneuvers designed to supple the horse,
bend him, teach him to move sideways from the rider's leg, and
eventually, to straighten him. Lateral movements contain varying
degrees of sideways movement. If you think of the most forward way
of traveling as walking in a straight line, then the most lateral way of
moving is moving directly sideways, as in a sidepass or full pass. In
between, there are variations such as western two-track, leg-yielding,
and the half-pass. Lateral movements also include exercises such as the
shoulder-in where the horse holds his body in a bent position while
moving forward, which causes him to cross one hind leg over the other
and one front leg over the other as he moves forward. The turn on the
forehand and the turn on the hindquarters can be thought of as variations
of lateral movements.

Although every lateral maneuver has different standards for the angle
and bend of the horse's body, neck, and throatlatch, and the degree of
collection and engagement, they do have one major characteristic in
common: The horse moves somewhat sideways and somewhat forward
at the same time. Most lateral movements are too advanced for the early
training of the young horse. Those that are appropriate to teach a young
horse are a turn on the forehand, leg-yield, and a large, gradual walk-
around turn on the hindquarters.

TURN ON THE FOREHAND

To help straighten a horse and to increase the engagement and activity of his hind legs, he must learn to yield to your lower legs. When you apply your left leg behind the girth, for example, the horse's hindquarters should move to the right. The degree of movement will depend on the regulation made by the reins and other aids.

To make yielding to the leg most clear, teach the horse the turn on the forehand sequence first. The turn on the forehand should be first attempted from the walk, then later from a halt. In the first phase, the walk-around turn on the forehand should be a long, low, sweeping turn so that the rhythm of the walk and the forward energy are not lost. It is a less-serious error for a horse to step forward with his front "pivot" foot when learning the turn on the forehand than it would be for him to step sideways with it. It is a serious error for him to step backward with any of his feet during a turn on the forehand. So keep the work very forward and do not cramp the young horse.

Ride clockwise (to the right) in an arena, off the rail about 6 feet. After the second corner of the short side, once your horse is going straight again, shift your weight to your left seat bone, apply your left leg well behind the girth and tip your horse's nose to the left asking him to swing his hindquarters to the right and swivel around on his front end. I have illustrated this in Figure 6. Turn 180 degrees so you are facing the opposite direction from where you started. Yield with the left rein to straighten the horse and walk straight ahead. After a few moments, change direction so that you can position him for another turn on the forehand. Practice two or three turns off your left leg before attempting turns off your right leg.

As the horse gains confidence and balance, you can move to Phase 2 in future lessons. Keeping your hands low, create a bend to the left with a slight left opening rein and a lightly supporting right rein. Then add your left seat bone and left leg behind the girth. This will cause the hindquarters to swing right. Allow the horse to step to the right with his right front leg so that he makes a small semicircle with his front legs (a larger one with his hind legs, see Figure 7).

Finally, in Phase 3, you will ask for a turn on the forehand on the spot—the horse will essentially walk around his relatively stationary left front leg (Figure 8). This means you will no longer allow him to step to the right with his right front leg. He must only step slightly forward with

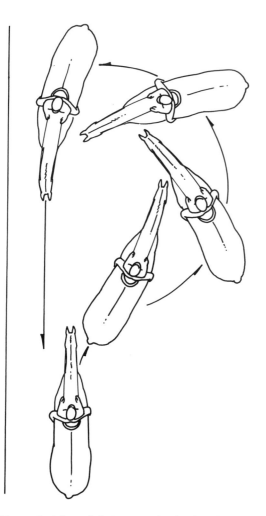

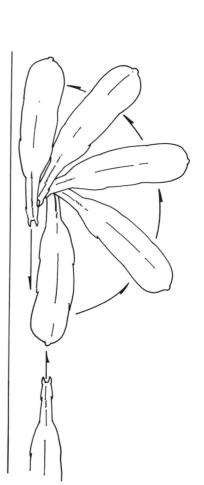

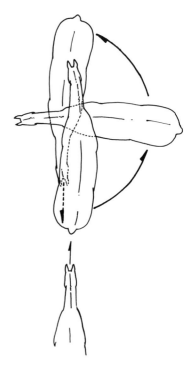

Figure 6. (above left) Turn on the forehand
stage 1.

Figure 7. (above right) Turn on the forehand
stage 2.

Figure 8. (right) Turn on the forehand stage 3.

88. In this, an early attempt at a turn on the forehand, the rider is using her right leg behind the cinch and the right direct rein. The horse's right hind leg has crossed so deeply over and in front of his left hind leg that it is stepping outside the left boundary of his body. The rider has made it clear that movement to the left is desired by taking the left leg off the horse. The rider should not be leaning so far to the right but should be sitting more directly over the horse.

89. A different view of a similar stage of the turn on the forehand. The left hind is uncrossing from behind the right hind and is getting ready to take a sideways step to the left. The left front will take a tiny step forward. The right front foot is the "pivot" foot.

it. You will regulate this with a more strongly supporting right rein which will prevent the horse from overbending to the left and popping out his right shoulder. In essence, you will be holding him straighter. At each moment that you apply the left leg (although maintaining a slight bend to the left with the left rein), lightly squeeze the right rein. If you feel a loss of forward energy, be sure you have not shortened the horse too much. You can use your right leg at the girth to create more forward motion. Remember, as the horse steps forward in response to your leg, yield with your hand. Practice the turn on the forehand in both directions. Photos 88 and 89 portray the turn in the opposite direction. It will take several weeks or more for you to go through the various stages of turn on the forehand in preparation for introducing the leg-yield.

Bending

Bending, often thought of as lateral flexion, customarily refers to the left or right curving of the horse's spine, but in actuality it is the shifting of the horse's weight to his left or right legs. Bending describes the arc made by the horse's body in a turn as would be evident in an aerial view. At first the young horse is asked to bend portions of his body—the throatlatch and the neck—in front of the rider's leg. Then the young horse is asked to bend his body around the rider's leg. This results in a shape somewhat like a comma where the horse's hindquarters are curled in the same direction as his head (photos 90 and 91). Concentrate on the position of your horse's hindquarters rather than his neck and you will have an easier time mastering bending and preventing overbending.

The reflex action to a bump or tap at the midpoint of a horse's ribs (especially when accompanied by a weighted seat bone on the same side) is a turning of his head and neck toward the tap and an arcing of the tail toward the tap. Therefore, rather than relying on tugs of the reins to bend a horse, use your lower legs and seat. Bending should be accomplished by using seat and leg aids first and rein aids second: Bend the horse from back to front rather than bending the front only as many riders tend to do. If you desire more bend in front, squeeze and release with the inside hand and use your inside seat bone. Keep contact with the outside rein so you can control the outside shoulder.

90. This two-year-old demonstrates an honest, supple turn creating an arc from his head to tail.

91. This stocky two-year-old bends at the throatlatch and turns her body in response to the rider's aids but because she is above the bit and less supple than the previous horse, her turn appears stiff.

Just as with humans, horses usually have a side preference. That is why most horses initially travel stiff, in one direction and overbent in the other. This is often referred to as a horse's natural stiffness and hollowness. Some horses are stiffer (stronger) on the left side of their bodies. That is, the left side of their bodies strongly resists stretching, so it stays rather flat. When traveling to the right for example, such a horse will have difficulty bending to the right. This will show up as the head carried to the left, the body held at an angle with the front feet outside the hind feet, the hindquarters shifted in to the right, weight falling out on the left shoulder. If asked to bend to the right, such a horse may finally overbend to the right and bulge (or pop) his left shoulder or hip out rather than evenly bending his entire body. When such a horse travels to the left, his strong left side may tend to overcurl him to the inside, and it might be difficult to keep him out on the right rein.

A crooked horse can throw a rider into a crooked position and vice versa (photo 92). A rider with a collapsed hip or twisted shoulders can

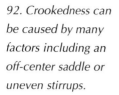

92. Crookedness can be caused by many factors including an off-center saddle or uneven stirrups.

perpetuate a horse's crookedness. The eventual goal is for the horse's body to travel in a relatively straight line. This will contribute to a rider's comfort and effectiveness. Straightening a horse, however, is a goal for the intermediate work, so do not attempt to work on it now. Keep the goal in mind, so that you know where you are headed and so you do not encourage the horse to develop an even more exaggerated tendency to his sidedness.

If you or your horse has a structural asymmetry, then it will be difficult to achieve balanced bending. Be aware of how your seat, legs, and upper body can affect a horse's lateral balance. If you ride with one stirrup longer than the other, it may cause you to throw the horse off balance. Over time the left stirrup leather stretches longer from mounting.

On the other hand, if you have one leg measurably longer than the other (rare), yet you force both legs to use equal stirrup lengths, you may be shifting your asymmetry up to your pelvis or spine. Or you may be putting a twist in the trunk of your body to compensate for the unevenness of your legs or stirrup leathers. Similarly, if a horse has a significant conformation asymmetry (and all do until they are sufficiently strengthened and straightened) it will be difficult for him to perform even the most basic bending exercises well. Asymmetric saddles can also cause or contribute to left-to-right balance problems. Throughout the basic training, never force yourself or your horse into an unnatural position. Gradually change things in a conservative manner.

Circles, Half-Turns, Serpentines, Figure Eights

Although it is ideal to ride the young horse on straight lines as much as possible until he can handle your weight, you will have to balance him from left to right using circular work (Figure 9). One of the best ways to work out stiffness and crookedness is to ride circles. Circles are the foundation of any horse's training program and are essential to most maneuvers. Three circle sizes you will use are:

66 feet (20m) in diameter: for walk, jog, posting trot, lope or
    canter
30 feet (9m) in diameter: for walk, jog, or posting trot
20 feet (6m) in diameter: for walk or jog

To help yourself visualize these sizes, set up cones or markers at measured distances or look at your arena rails, which commonly are 10 feet long. The length of two standard rails will be the approximate width (diameter) of a 20-foot circle. When working in an arena on a 20m (66 foot) circle, imagine you are riding in a full-sized round pen.

You will work the young horse mostly in large circles, but in his hollow direction you might find he curls up and the circle gets very small. Your goal is to have him keep the bend to the inside but to keep his weight up on the outside rein so that you can maintain the large circle size. This may require you to ride him straight or even slightly counterflexed until he gains his balance (photos 93, 94, and 95). The body of a counter-flexed horse is in relatively the same position as it would be if he was bent to the inside. By using a stronger outside rein, however, you keep the horse from overbending his neck to the inside and falling

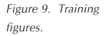

*Figure 9. Training
figures.*

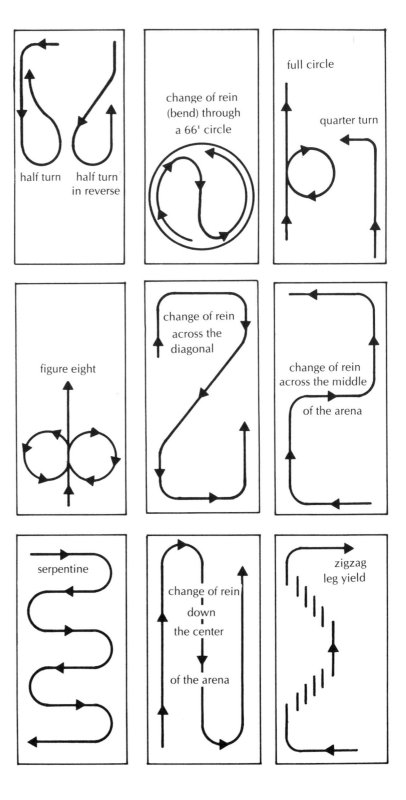

93. On a large circle to the right, the horse's throatlatch is bent to the right, into the direction of movement.

94. On the same circle to the right, the horse is kept straight.

95. On the same circle to the right, the horse's throatlatch is counterbent (often called counterflexed) to the left.

on his inside shoulder. After working a horse in a slightly counter-flexed 66-foot circle, ride him straight in the same sized circle. Finally, add the inside bend. This may take a month or more to accomplish as it requires muscle retraining and strengthening.

Once the horse is securely on the outside rein and bent to the inside you can spiral him from a large circle to a medium circle (and vice versa) without the horse falling in on his forehand. (See spiraling and turn on the hindquarters in Chapter 6.)

Tear-drop shaped half-turns (reverses), half-turns in reverse, arcing turns in the corner of the arena, serpentines, and figure eights all have circular components. Riding a horse in various sizes and shapes of circular maneuvers will show you his tendencies to drop in, drift out, come above or behind the bit, stiffen or collapse. Then you can use your aids and exercises to help him overcome these imbalances. With circular work, emphasize the use of your seat and legs rather than the reins.

Use serpentines to really make the connection clear in the horse's mind between your seat and turning. When turning left, use left seat bone and left leg to arc the horse's body to the left. As you approach the straight portion of the serpentine, ride very symmetrically and very forward, weight even on both seat bones. Then shift to the right seat bone, right leg; straighten again when between loops and so on. The balance in your seat is your key to power steering.

Eventually when you come to a corner of the arena you will want to adjust your aids so that you can negotiate the turn with your horse remaining balanced. This requires an effective use of the outside aids which will be emphasized in later training.

At this point, you might decide to:
1. turn the horse out for several months or the winter,
2. continue working on previous lessons to strengthen the horse mentally and physically or,
3. go on with the training progression.

Leg-Yielding

The goal of a leg-yield is to further develop obedience to the lateral aids at the walk and trot. Lateral aids refer to aids applied on the same side of the horse's body. So, similarly to the turn on the forehand and in very

simple terms, for a leg-yield to the right the predominant aids will be left rein, left leg; for a leg-yield to the left, the predominant aids will be right rein, right leg (photo 96 and 97). While a turn on the forehand results in a reverse of direction, the leg-yield results in continued motion in the same direction. The horse's body is positioned at a 30- to 45-degree angle to the side of the arena or to an imaginary straight line of forward travel. The horse's spine is straight, which results in forward and sideways movement and a crossing over of his legs.

For a leg-yield to the right (Figure 10), the left rein creates very slight bend to the left. The left leg behind the girth asks the hindquarters to move to the right, the left hind stepping deep under and in front of the right hind. The right hind will uncross from behind the left hind and step sideways and so on. The left seat bone assists the rider's left leg, and in fact, later takes over the predominant aiding role from the leg by pushing on the left side of the horse's spine sideways to the right. The timing for the use of the seat bone and lower leg is critical. It must occur just as the left hind leg is reaching under. This will accent and intensify the reach, resulting in greater lateral movement (a larger sideways step).

96. (above left) Early leg yielding at the walk: The horse is yielding to the rider's right leg and moving forward and to the left. The right hind (dark leg) has just crossed over and in front of the left hind (white sock).

97. (above right) The right front has crossed over and in front of the left front; the left hind is un-crossing from behind the right hind.

Figure 10. Leg-yield

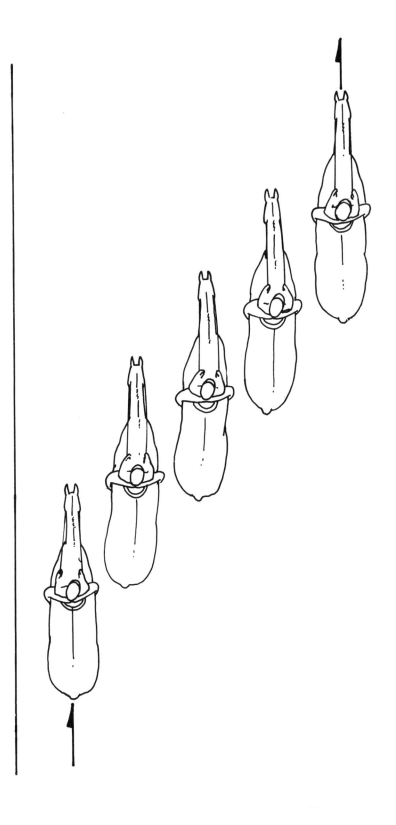

You should apply a distinct set of aids for each sideways step that you request, therefore there will be a slight rocking motion in your pelvis as you encourage the horse to take a series of steps sideways. Try to keep your legs even, otherwise the one predominantly aiding may tend to get lower and lower resulting in a slipped saddle, a collapsed hip, or a crooked upper body. Do not ask for too much bend with the left rein. Keep your right rein ready to check any popping out of the right shoulder which is often caused by too much bend to the left. To correct an overbent horse, ride the horse actively forward for a moment, soften the left rein, straighten the horse with the right rein and then resume the movement. The right leg remains lightly on the horse at the girth, but it is passive unless it is required to remind the horse to continue moving forward. Then it can be used in a squeezing or bumping fashion.

The leg-yield can be performed on a circle at a walk and along the rail (photo 98) or across a diagonal of the arena at a walk or trot (photo 99). It should be practiced a few steps at a time giving the horse a chance to build up the strength required for the exercise. Leg-yielding can provide many benefits for the developing horse. However, if practiced

98. (below left) Here the young horse leg-yields in a straight line along the rail. However there is too much inside bend.

99. (below right) During the leg-yield to the left at the trot, the right hind and left front reach energetically forward and sideways.

incorrectly or for too long, it can cause great problems later on. Use leg-yielding as a means to an end, a temporary stage to help you put your horse on the aids. Eventually you will want your horse to bend at the throatlatch *into* the direction of movement during lateral work and not hold his body at the exaggerated angle of leg-yielding.

Leg-yielding on a circle at the walk provides added benefit because you can begin to add inside bending to the movement. On a 20-meter circle, first establish inside bend with the inside rein and let the horse relax. Then gradually establish contact with the outside rein all the time being sure the horse is staying forward on the circle and remains bent to the inside. Then apply the inside seat bone and leg to accent the sideways reaching of the inside hind leg. Do this very slowly so you can identify errors and correct them. If the horse quickens instead of stepping more deeply under, you may have to review the turn on the forehand to be sure the horse knows that your leg behind the girth (along with the supporting action of the outside rein) means more sideways movement, not a quickened pace.

Canter

Once a horse has learned the rudiments of leg aids, he is ready to canter. Of course, you can canter your horse before this time but if you have any problems, you won't have the means to correct them. So I suggest you wait until you have the ability to position the horse's hindquarters with your legs before you canter him. That way, cantering will probably occur naturally and balanced and you will have no major problems.

The canter or lope is a three-beat gait that begins with one hind leg, followed by a diagonal pair, and ends with the leading foreleg. So, if the initiating hind leg is the left, the diagonal pair will consist of the right hind and the left front, and the leading foreleg will be the right front and the horse will be on the right lead (photo 100). When observing a horse on the right lead from the side, his right legs will reach farther forward than the left legs. The right hind will reach under his belly farther forward than the left hind; the right front will reach out in front of his body farther than the left front.

If a horse is on the left lead, the situation reverses: the initiating hind is the right hind, followed by the diagonal pair (left hind/right front) and finished by the left front (photo 101). The canter has an alternating

100. This is an energetic yet fairly balanced canter for a young horse. Notice that the croup is lower than the fore-hand and the inside hind leg is driving far up under the horse's belly. The right lead: the left hind is supporting all of the weight; the diagonal pair (right hind and left front) are gliding in for landing while the lead foreleg (right front) is beginning to uncurl and swing forward.

101. Young horses should be allowed to lope actively forward and elevate their heads if necessary to keep their balance. Later in their training and conditioning, they can be asked to lope with a some-what lower head carriage if desired. Approximately the same moment as the previous photo but on the left lead.

rolling and floating feeling to it. The energy rolls from rear to front, then during a moment of suspension, the horse gathers his legs underneath himself to get organized for the next set of leg movements and the rider seems to glide for a moment until the initiating hind lands and begins the cycle again. You can see this sequence in photos 102, 103, and 104.

For a horse to be balanced, especially in the lope, when the leading foreleg hits the ground, the horse must be driven forward and allowed

102. A non-interfering rider at the lope on a two-year-old (whose typically higher croup at this age causes her to be somewhat heavier on the forehand). During the downswing, the weight is mostly borne by the leading foreleg. Although this rider offers light support through the reins, she does not pull on them.

103. The gathering phase where the hind legs are coming back under the body. The rider sits deep.

104. Just before the moment of suspension when all of the legs are off the ground, the rider sits light, allowing the young horse to rebalance under her. Very soon, the left hind leg will initiate the sequence again.

to use his head and neck freely (with the head slightly up if necessary) to keep from falling heavily on the forehand. With the neck slightly curved and the poll even with the top of the withers (or 3 to 4 inches above or below depending on the horse's conformation), and the head at the vertical or several degrees in front of the vertical, a horse is able to bring his hind legs underneath his belly. A horse that is allowed or forced to carry his head lower and his neck flatter (by use of a running martingale, side reins, or relentless hands) than is natural for his conformation may tend to compensate for the imbalance by traveling "strung-out" behind: the hind end trailing too far behind the body, rather than working up underneath it. Moving strung-out also tends to break up the diagonal pair of legs at the lope, resulting in a disjointed gait—the rear is not in sync with the front end. If a horse is slowed down too much, the diagonal pair can break and begin landing separately, giving rise to a four-beat lope where the horse appears to be loping in front and jogging behind. On the other hand, if a horse is ridden with a very short rein and is pulled up tight to canter, his back will be tense, unable to round and will tend to be rigidly hollow with a high head carriage (photo 105). Remember your goal is a free, forward canter.

To make it easiest for a young horse to canter on the correct lead, ask for the canter from an energetic but balanced trot. I suggest you post until two strides before you ask for the canter. Then you should sit the trot, position the horse, and ask for the depart.

Position him systematically so that the canter evolves from a set of preparatory aids rather than a sudden surprise. First tip the horse's nose to the inside but not so far that his outside shoulder bulges causing him to take the outside lead. Support the action of the inside rein with the outside rein. Then move his hindquarters to the outside by using your

105. The horse that canters rigidly with no supple rounding of his topline has a tense, hollow back, with trailing hindquarters and braced neck.

inside leg behind the cinch and remind his outside shoulder to stay contained by squeezing with your outside hand. This pre-canter positioning is similar to leg-yielding.

Now he is positioned and prepared for the depart aids. Do not hold him in this preparatory position for longer than a stride or two because he may tend to shorten, quicken, and get tense. The transition should be smooth, slow, and forward. If you feel the stride shortening or tension building, release the preparatory aids, ride him forward at a posting trot and start again. You can let him trot with a long stride but do not let him trot with a quick rhythm.

When you are ready to ask for the depart, weight your inside seat bone, move your inside leg forward to its normal position, let your inside seat bone move forward too, and move your outside leg back in order to position the hindquarters underneath the horse. Keep your shoulders back and lift your ribcage. This will cause the horse to canter, taking his first canter step forward with the outside hind leg and then driving deeply with the inside hind leg.

Whether you are riding western or English, you will probably find the best success cantering from a posting trot (as described above with a few steps of sitting trot just before you depart). Once you can accomplish departs using the posting trot sequence, you can attempt them from the sitting trot or jog and later on from the walk. But these departs require that the horse is accustomed to the use of half halts and the action of the outside rein and is sufficiently strong on both hind legs. So these advanced departures are more appropriate for a later stage of the horse's training.

Remember, for a smooth, hind leg first canter depart, your seat must be the primary aid. Don't lean your upper body forward in an attempt to urge the horse into a canter. This just throws the horse onto his forehand and may cause the horse to fall into a front leg first canter. Don't rock or pump with your body in an attempt to maintain the canter as this too will negatively affect the horse's balance. To follow and maintain the elementary canter, your inside hand, leg, and seat bone should be appropriately active and follow the motion of the horse while your outside hand, leg, and seat bone should tend to be steady.

A good exercise for young horses is to strike a canter from a large circle, go to the arena at large for one time around (or less), make another large circle and drop to a trot in the circle or just after the circle joins the arena rail. The canter-to-trot transitions should be really forward—

the horse should not shut down, letting his nose take a dive and his croup pop up. Sit deep especially on the outside seat bone and encourage him to wind down by rounding his back and bringing his hind legs well underneath himself. In order to do this, he will have to be allowed to use his neck freely to balance himself. At first you may need to allow a horse to trot quite energetically for a few strides after the downward transition so he can dissipate his momentum as he regains his balance. Eventually he will develop the strength and balance necessary to move from a canter into a quiet trot (or walk) by rounding his topline, shifting his weight to his hindquarters. But this takes weeks of muscle training and hind leg strengthening.

Once a young horse can lope or canter for three or four minutes without a break, begin testing his self-carriage and rhythm by periodically feeding him a longer rein. He may fall a little on his forehand but his rhythm should remain the same. Gather him up and rebalance him, then check again. By the end of the first year he should be able to canter in balance and in rhythm both on and off contact.

PROBLEMS WITH THE CANTER

Often things will go along pretty smoothly until you begin working on the canter. Some of the most common problems are when a horse won't canter, canters on the wrong lead, or runs away. In general, it is best to go back and review all past work at the walk and trot for several weeks, and when you return to the canter you will probably find that the problem has solved itself.

For a horse that won't canter, be sure you aren't restraining him too much with the inside rein as this will block his inside shoulder. If that's not the cause of the problem, it might be that you are holding him in the preparatory position too long and you lose his forward movement. Or perhaps your aids aren't distinct enough. Be sure you are moving your inside hip forward enough. Don't resort to just using an outside leg to ask for a canter as you won't be positioning the horse properly. You will, in effect, be cueing your horse, but not aiding him.

If a young horse takes a wrong lead, don't make a big deal out of it. If you are riding out, just go with the wrong lead for a bit unless it will cause the horse to be unbalanced. If you are riding in a round pen or in an arena where you will have to turn on the wrong lead, quietly drop to a trot, trot until he is relaxed, then set him up and ask again. If the wrong lead is a consistent problem, review bending exercises being sure that the horse is in a true bend around the inside leg. Review leg-yielding so that you are able to properly position the horse. Be sure that you are sitting squarely in the saddle and your stirrups are the same length. If the problem persists, try from a posting trot; try it by posting on the *wrong* diagonal and give the depart aids as you sit. You might also find success by cantering after an extreme inside bend in a corner or after a small circle.

If a horse canters disunited, (canters on one lead behind and the other in front), he was likely crooked at the time of departure. He may need more bending, suppling, or leg-yielding exercises to prepare him for cantering on his difficult side. Going disunited can also be caused by a release of a rein or leg aid at the moment of departure when that aid should be held. Often the young horse depends on the aids for balance and if you let go at just the wrong instance will cause him to fall out somewhere and get crooked. A rider with a collapsed side or hip can also cause a horse to have difficulty with one or both leads.

If a horse runs when asked to canter, you can go back to the ground work or you can deal with it in the saddle. If you are able to sit still and not pull, you can ride it out until the horse needs a brief break, then you can canter again. If it looks like his running away is going to get you in trouble, use the double. Doubling is a way of taking hold of a horse by grabbing the inside rein close up to the bit and pulling the horse into a tight circle. This will make him slow down but it could also cause him to fall or resist strongly by rearing. Therefore, keep you hand low, but don't let your weight get thrown too far to the inside or you may pop off in the middle of the whirlwind. Once the horse has quieted down, release the doubling rein and go on as if nothing has happened.

6

Moving On, Riding Out

THE FOURTH THROUGH TWELFTH MONTHS
Contact and Connection

At first the young horse was just required to accept the presence of the bit, saddle, and rider. Then he learned to respond to your aids. As his lessons progress, he will need to accept *contact* with your aids. Contact refers to the amount of pressure that is felt between the horse and the rider through seat (and horse's back), legs (and horse's sides), and reins (horse's mouth). I have illustrated this in photo 106 and Figure 11. Some people erroneously think that contact refers only to the relationship between the horse's mouth and the rider's hands through the reins. But contact is greatly dependant on the horse accepting the rider's weight and legs. In fact, contact should result *more* from seat and leg aids than rein aids. It should be achieved by a stronger engagement of the hindquarters rather than a pulling back on the reins. Your lower legs should drive the horse up to an optimum rein length. The rein contact is not let up but it is not pulled either. The reins are handled with a very steady, but elastic feel as if they were side reins. Once the boundary has been set, the horse should be invited to fill it up. Each time a horse works within a new degree of contact, you should yield momentarily with the reins. Contact is not an all-or-nothing lesson. It is a gradual building up and containing of energy that spans several years. Develop contact by degrees.

In order for a connection to be useful, you must sit evenly in the saddle and hold the reins evenly and steadily so that what you create in the hindquarters doesn't leak out of the ribs, shoulders, neck, or nose. Hold the horse's ribs in position with your legs. Gradually develop a coil spring between your driving aids and your restraining aids. At first when horses resist contact they try to find an escape route. But if you are consistent and fair a horse will accept the new level of pressure you have introduced. Once he accepts the pressure, yield with both hands and let him momentarily reach forward and/or down toward the ground so he can round his topline. (But don't let the reins go slack or you will have lost what you have gained.) Then reestablish the contact and try to create the rounding of the topline.

As a horse begins rounding underneath me and into my hands, it feels like I am sitting on a bow that is being strung beneath me. The bow is the horse's spine from his nose to his tail. The imaginary bow string runs from the horse's mouth along the horse's sides and attaches to his tail. At first the string is either very slack or it has become tightened incorrectly because the bow has bent backwards (the horse has hollowed his topline). However, once an elastic connection has been made between the driving aids and the rein aids, you can gradually tighten the string a notch at a time and cause the horse to round his topline. If you have ever practiced archery, you know that a strung bow has a tremendous amount of power and energy while an unstrung bow is ineffective and weak. If you string your horse correctly it will feel like you are sitting on top of a resilient arc that contracts and expands in

Figure 11. (left) Degree of contact is initiated by all of the rider's aids and the net result is the degree of energy and carriage of the horse. (K.D. Blackwell)

106. Contact refers to the relationship between the transmission and reception of pressure from the rider's seat, legs, and hands to the horse's back, sides, and mouth.

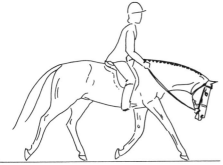

flowing motions and has plenty of energy ready for you to use. Only require the developing horse to remain "strung" for moments at a time. Ask for increases very gradually over a reasonable period of time. Think of your own training and development. If you were out of shape and went to a coach who on the first day required you to do 100 straight-legged situps with your arms behind your head, by about situp number twenty you might be getting pretty sore in your lower back and maybe harboring some pretty resentful thoughts about the coach's unfair expectations. Ask for reasonable efforts from the horse and reward him frequently with stretch and rest breaks.

Later in a horse's development, you can offer him a different type of reward for his acceptance of contact by releasing the inside rein somewhat so he can stretch down while maintaining contact on the outside rein. If it is time during the lesson for a more substantial break, let him stretch the reins out of your hands for about a minute, making sure you can always feel him on the end of the long rein. Then gradually reel him in and go back to work. Momentary yielding should be on-going throughout a training session. Stretch breaks may need to come every 3 or 4 minutes at first and at least every 10 to 15 minutes for a horse in any stage of development.

Now that the horse has become familiar with leg aids and contact, you can begin riding corners and circles differently. As you approach a turn, instead of weighting the inside stirrup, weight the inside seat bone and put a strong inside leg on the horse in the middle position. Set an appropriate amount of contact with the outside rein and let the inside rein and leg softly talk to the horse's mouth and side with an active invitation to bend at the jaw, poll, and body against the supporting outside rein as you move through the corner. Keep the outside leg on as needed to keep the horse moving forward and the horse's shoulder from popping outward. As you finish the corner, straighten your seat, maintain even pressure with both legs at the girth, quiet the inside rein and straighten the horse up with the outside rein and ride straight forward.

Contact before, during, and after a corner should be even, smooth, and steady. Wavering contact, caused by rider imbalance, can create a bumping in the horse's mouth, a banging on the horse's back, and a slapping of the horse's sides, all of which interrupt the horse's ability to move smoothly and carry himself in a balanced fashion.

The steadier the contact is with your seat, legs, and hands, the better chance you will have at developing a harmonious connection between your driving aids and your restraining aids. You use your seat, legs, upper body, and weight to encourage a horse to move forward and you use your seat, lower legs, and hands to restrain and shape the energy you have created with your driving aids. That solid, uninterrupted feeling of energy flow through your body and the horse's is often referred to as the connection. It is as if the trainer is plugged into the horse. The horse that is well-connected drives powerfully yet fluidly from the hindquarters sending the energy up to a well-hinged forehand—one where the neck is carried from the muscles which attach at the vertebrae of the withers.

DEGREE OF CONTACT

The degree of contact that you will employ in the training of your young horse will vary according to your riding style and the proficiency of your aids, the conformation of the horse, and the stage of his training. Various types of riding refer to contact in different ways—taking a hold, a light feel, on the bit, in the bridle, and up in the bridle. Trainers using a slack rein, such as is characteristic in western riding, aim for a very light contact. The degree of contact for a well-trained western horse, ideally, is based on very small movements of the reins and their subtle action on the lips, tongue, and bars of the horse's mouth as well as a light touch of the reins on the horse's neck. The reason well-trained western horses can be controlled on a slack rein is because they have been previously trained to respond to the rider's weight, seat, and legs as primary cues. A poorly trained western horse, however, can have a horrible time if his trainer has not prepared him with body cues and tries to ride on loose rein cues alone. Every time the horse gets out of position or rhythm, instead of making adjustments with seat and legs, such a rider picks up the reins and causes the bit to bump the horse's mouth. Often this is an abrupt surprise to the horse and soon the horse approaches his work with suspicion and tension.

Horses ridden with a shorter rein, such as is characteristic in hunt seat or dressage, often feel a greater degree of constant pressure on the lips, tongue, and bars from the bit. Theoretically, this allows a rider to make more subtle adjustments when applying rein aids. The goal of classical dressage is lightness and self-carriage, but as with all forms of riding it is easy to forget the goal. Riding with a too-strong contact on the reins seems to naturally lead to the bad habit of the rider pulling on the reins and the horse reciprocating by bracing stiffly on the bit. Or, once the rider has the horse in a desired form, instead of softening the aids (releasing), the rider holds steadily on the reins and causes the horse to lean on the rider's aids. A horse ridden in such a way will never develop self-carriage. He will always have to be forcibly held together.

RESPONSE TO PRESSURE

Horses resist heavy, steady pressure and yield to light, intermittent pressure. That means if you are trying to get a horse to respond in his jaw and poll to your hands on the reins and you pull steadily and with great force on both reins, the horse will likely try to push into and out of that pressure, using the underside of his neck to resist your strong rein aid. If, on the other hand, you hold a steady pressure on one rein (usually the outside rein) and use a light squeeze and release action on the inside rein, the horse will likely yield to that action in his mouth; he will flex at the poll and in his lower jaw in response to the light, intermittent pressure on the bars of his mouth. Once a horse has responded this way, the rein contact should become steady but very light.

The same pressure principle applies to the use of your seat and legs and to the overall use of your body when you are on the ground. When riding, if you drive rigidly with your seat onto the horse's back, he will probably tense and/or hollow his back in a form of protective resistance. If you use your seat in a firm way followed by a yielding once the horse complies or in a series of light, intermittent collecting movements followed by a quiet following seat, the horse will respond and begin moving with a more rounded topline.

Leg pressure works in a similar fashion and is based on work from the ground. When trying to get a horse to move his body away from hand pressure when you are on the ground, if you lean your full weight into the horse, steadily and with all your might, the horse will probably lean back into you. If, on the other hand, you use little taps with your fingertips or small bumps with the base of your hand on the horse's side, he will move away from the pressure. When you are mounted, you will find that intermittent bumps with your lower legs are often more effective in obtaining the desired response from your horse than is a steady grip.

Before rein contact is really brought to issue, the horse must have well-established energy from the hindquarters. You will shape this energy with your leg and weight aids and signals to the bit. If you do nothing of consequence with the bridle and just sit in the middle of the horse as a passive passenger, the horse will likely travel relatively relaxed but strung out. If you attempt to gain rein contact abruptly or incorrectly by pulling on the reins, a horse may hollow its back and either bob its head up and down searching for a steady feel or come above the bit, holding its head and neck in a rigid, unyielding configuration (photo 107).

When a horse raises its head above the vertical, it often does so by pushing out muscles on the underside of the neck, which hollows the top of the neck. This can result in a permanent upside-down neck shape. One of the reasons a horse inverts is to shift the bit from the sensitive bars to the less sensitive corners of the mouth. When resisting or evading the horse elects to take the pressure, whether it be a heavy steady pull or incessant jerking, on the corner of the lips and the premolars rather than on the sensitive bars. A hollow back usually accompanies this neck carriage and is another way of the horse resisting contact (from a thumping rider's seat).

107. A horse which has come above the bit in a stiff unyielding configuration.

108. A horse which has dropped behind the bit and behind the vertical is avoiding contact.

Another means of avoiding contact is when a horse gets behind the bit (photo 108). Horses with lovely, sculptured necks and neat throat-latches as well as horses that are extremely sensitive or afraid of the bit can get behind the bit in an attempt to escape the rider's aids. Behind the bit is often but not always the same as behind the vertical.

IS YOUR YOUNG HORSE CORRECTLY ON THE BIT? (Photo 109)

Is the poll the highest point of his neck?

Is his nose 5 to 20 degrees in front of the vertical?

When turning does your horse bend at the jaw, poll, and body or does he avoid proper bending by bending at the middle of his neck and keeping his body stiff?

Is the rein contact steady on the outside rein?

Can you give slack to the inside rein and still maintain bend and tempo?

Does his mouth foam and slobber because his salivary glands below his ears are stimulated from active engagement and a proper head carriage?

If a horse's nose is not perpendicular to the ground but rather is carried closer to the chest, the horse is termed "behind the vertical." If a horse is in a behind-the-vertical configuration and the reins are loose

109. A young horse that is on the bit rounds down into even contact while moving actively forward.

with no contact to the rider's hand, the horse is also "behind the bit." (For that matter, if a horse's nose is on or in front of the vertical and the reins are loose, the horse is not considered to be "on the bit" for hunter or dressage riding even though the same frame and rein contact might be considered appropriate contact for a western horse.)

If, on the other hand, the horse is behind the vertical and the reins are relatively taut, the horse *might* be on the bit. Only the rider knows for sure because it is a matter of feel. However, even if the behind-the-vertical horse *is* on the bit, such a configuration is *not* desirable because the horse is so restricted he cannot move freely. Sometimes such a stage

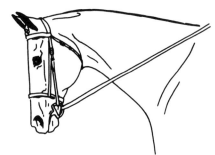

moderate to strong contact;
may or may not be on the bit;
at the vertical.
(ok for intermediate English horse
provided horse is on the bit)

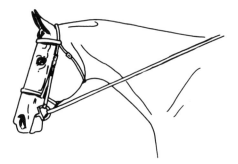

moderate to strong contact;
may or may not be on the bit;
in front of the vertical.
(desirable for beginning English horse)

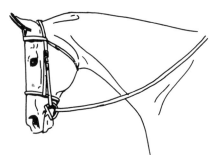

light contact;
may or may not be on the bit;
at the vertical.
(ok for intermediate western horse
provided horse does not get behind the bit)

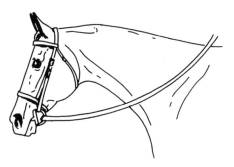

light contact;
may or may not be on the bit;
in front of the vertical.
(desirable for beginning western horse)

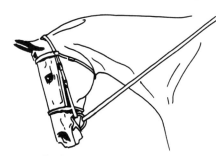

strong contact;
could be on the bit but probably
behind the bit;
behind the vertical.
(not desirable)

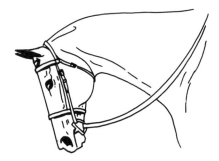

no contact;
behind the bit;
behind the vertical.
(not desirable)

Figure 12. Is your horse on the bit? (K.D. Blackwell)

is necessary (at least temporarily) when initially making a point with a horse about accepting contact with the bit (Figure 12). But such a technique should only be used by a very experienced trainer. At the same time the horse is learning to accept contact and flexion, he should be driven up strongly from behind, which will make it easier for him to accept the bit and to reach forward as he moves. At each instance of compliance, the horse should be rewarded with a softening of the aids. The goal is a lengthening and lowering of the entire frame, not just the forehand.

IS YOUR HORSE ON THE AIDS?

(This is more advanced than on the bit because it includes more advanced responses to weight, back, and leg aids.)

Does your horse move forward when you close both legs at the cinch?

Does your horse move sideways when a leg is used behind the cinch?

Does your horse listen to your seat for slowing down, turning, connecting?

Does your horse understand moving longer without moving faster? (extension)

Does your horse understand moving shorter without necessarily moving slower? (collection)

Longitudinal Flexion and Balance

Flexion usually refers to movement of the spine and limbs in the vertical plane. It includes flexion of the joints of the horse's lower jaw, poll, neck at the withers, back, and croup as well as flexion of the joints of the legs. Flexion is essential for the development of collection, impulsion, and animation, which are qualities beyond the scope of a horse's early training but are goals to keep in mind.

Flexion also is essential for the development of longitudinal balance, however, which in its elementary form *is* part of the young horse's training. Longitudinal balance primarily relates to the working relationship between the front portion of the horse and the rear portion of the horse. Because the majority of a horse's weight is in his forehand, left to his own devices he would probably travel more heavily on his forehand because of the simple fact that it is easier. It requires less work on his part to leave the weight forward where it naturally settles rather than rebalance the weight to the rear and carry it with the hindquarters. When you ride a horse that is extremely heavy on the forehand, you will find that such a manner of travel is labored and not comfortable. You will probably feel like you are sliding downhill or your arms are being pulled forward, which in turn lifts your seat out of the saddle. Besides being labored, heavy-on-the-forehand horses seem to suffer a great number and intensity of front leg lamenesses.

So the goal, for your sake and your horse's, is to gradually convince the young horse to shift his balance rearward and carry more of his weight with his hind legs. This will give you a more comfortable place to sit—a still spot in the center of the motion of the horse's body, something like the quiet at the center of a teeter-totter. To provide you with a comfortable place in the center of motion, your horse will need to be convinced that he can and should carry more of his weight (and yours) with his hindquarters. This takes training and conditioning so that the horse can develop the necessary muscles to be able to carry himself in more desirable balance. When we have achieved this with a horse, we have positively altered the horse's longitudinal or anterior/posterior balance.

Advanced Bending

In initial bending work, the horse was asked to respond to the inside (opening) rein and bend around your inside leg. Perhaps you stepped lightly into the inside stirrup. The outside hand was giving and the outside leg was passive. Now in elementary flexion work, you will add a more active influence from the outside rein and outside leg and you will use your weight to the inside in a more distinct fashion. Now, instead of just stepping into the inside stirrup, you more actively use a shift of weight to your inside seat bone to initiate and hold a bend. You can further amplify your weight aid by turning your hips in the direction of the turn which makes your outside seat bone move ahead of your inside seat bone.

An increase of pressure on the outside rein asks for more flexion in the lower jaw and poll. Moving the outside leg behind the girth and using it actively rather than passively results in the rear half of the horse's spine being held straight or wrapping around your inside leg. (So, instead of just the front of the horse curling to the inside, the rear of the horse curls to the inside as well.) The purpose of the outside leg at this level of training, however, is to just hold the hindquarters straight behind the front end. Sometimes you may need to exaggerate the aids to show your horse he is capable of curling his hindquarters inward. Then when you moderate your request and only ask him to keep his hindquarters straight, it will seem "easier" to him.

Outside aids on a circle

Introduce the outside aids only after the horse has learned the inside aids. You introduced outside aids by riding your horse a little deeper into arena corners. Now, develop the use of the outside aids gradually on a circle. Start with a regular bend to the inside of the circle using leg and rein. The outside rein first serves to limit the bend but eventually takes over as the main rein effect. The horse should learn to maintain the inside bend and stay up on the outside rein. Periodically as the horse moves correctly, lighten the inside rein and check to see if the horse has yet developed any degree of self-carriage. He may be able to hold himself in the correct bend for a stride or two and then before he falls apart (and starts counter-flexing), add the inside leg and inside rein once again. Add your outside leg behind the middle position to bend the rear half of the spine toward the inside of the circle just a tiny bit, taking care not to let the horse tip his nose to the outside which would let slack fall into the outside rein.

Spirals

Now make the circle smaller by riding the horse forward and into the outside rein and using the outside leg at or slightly in front of the middle position to help turn the horse to the inside. If you try to pull the horse around into a smaller circle with the inside rein, you will probably just succeed in popping his outside shoulder (and perhaps his hindquarters) to the outside of the circle. If the horse gets tense, go back to riding the larger circle and reviewing positioning. The outside aids create a boundary within which the horse must work. Let him discover the boundary without fear and let him develop a physical acceptance of it gradually.

Besides the suppling and straightening benefits, adding the outside aids begins strengthening the horse's hind legs. It brings the outside hind leg up under the horse's body instead of letting it drift to the outside where it can avoid the more difficult work of carrying in addition to its normal driving role. When a hind leg is directly under the horse's body, the joints must flex to a greater degree and the muscles must subsequently work harder.

Half Halt/Check

The half halt (dressage) or check (western) is a means of calling a horse to attention, of heightening his awareness, and organizing him. It can be applied lightly or quite strongly. In the later stages of the initial training of a young horse, this preparatory exercise should be used before and after both upward and downward transitions because it prepares the horse for what is to come. A half halt also will allow you to balance the horse before asking the horse for an increase or decrease in tempo or length of stride. Using half halts properly improves a horse's balance and encourages self-carriage.

A half halt begins with the driving influence from the rider's deepened seat, an influencing seat that results from flexed abdominals, which cause the seat bones to move forward and be still and the lower back to flatten. Because this is the way you taught your horse to slow down and halt, the horse should respond by driving underneath himself deeper.

At the same time, your lower legs are applied actively in the middle position to cause the horse to step energetically forward. Simultaneously, the reins are held evenly and firmly so that the result is a momentary compacting of the horse's body: a bowing upward of the back, a slight rounding of the neck to counterbalance the increased deepness of the hindquarters caused by flexion of the loin.

The instant a positive response is felt, both the driving and restraining aids should be lightened taking care not to lose what has been gained but encouraging the horse to hold the energized and rounder shape by himself (self-carriage). Now the horse is in an ideal configuration and a primed state of energy to make whatever change you request.

The seat, back, and lower legs are all essential aids for a half halt or check; however, the rein aids provide a clearer means to explain the degrees of intensity possible in a half halt. The amount of pressure that should be applied with the reins will depend on the level of the horse's training and his expected response. In the earliest stages, a mere closing of the fingers on the reins may be required. Or it may be more appropriate to use a slight rolling inward of the fists, the hands curling at the wrists. In some cases, it may be necessary to actually take back with a movement in the upper arm. And in extreme instances (to make sure that a half halt will go through) a rider may have to take back with the upper arm and even lean back with the upper body. A more forceful half halt can be used occasionally to show a horse that he must listen to your aids but should be reserved for strategically planned instances. To retain response and lightness, after using a major half halt, lessen the intensity of subsequent half halts to the lowest level possible. During all instances, the seat, back, and lower legs should be applied with a greater intensity than that of the rein aids.

Canter to trot
The half halt is an essential portion of the downward transition from canter to trot. As the horse is cantering, you prepare for the transition by changing your leg position (from outside leg back to both legs on the girth) and no longer follow the canter movement with your seat. Make it obvious to the horse that you have stopped following his cantering movement by flexing your abdominals, steadying your seat (slightly more weight on your outside seat bone), but keeping your lower legs on. As soon as he begins trotting, yield to his forward motion with the reins and change your seat from a still seat to a normal, following trot seat. You may need to check the horse at every stride until he is trotting quietly.

Rating or speed control
Another use of the half halt is for speed control. When you want to slow down or rate your horse, that is shorten his stride or slow his tempo, accomplish it with a series of half halts applied at the moment of suspension. During the canter this moment comes right after the leading foreleg lands and the hind legs are reaching forward under the horse. At the trot this moment comes twice during each stride as each diagonal pair lifts. When applying a series of half halts to rate a horse, be sure there is a release after each successful reaction. Do not be tempted to hold on to what you gain and think you can build a lighter, rounder, or slower (more collected) horse by holding. You *must* yield after each half

halt compliance. And be sure that your seat and outside aids are the predominant aids used. If you overemphasize the inside aids, the horse will be over bent, will break somewhere along the outside, and there will be an energy leak—the half halts will not go through.

Lengthening and Shortening the Stride
An effective half halt teaches the horse the difference between pushing with the hindquarters and carrying with them. For both extension and collection, the horse must learn to carry more weight on his hindquarters. Teaching a horse to lenghten his gaits is valuable whether the horse is destined to be a ranch horse, a hunter, or a dressage horse. One of the clearest ways to teach a horse to move out is to move from a jog (or sitting trot) into a posting trot. If you drive with your seat and squeeze with both legs at the girth each time you sit, it will energize the horse's hind legs and make them reach farther forward. As you rise, the horse's unconstrained back is better able to bow upward. Keep your hands low for lengthening, especially the outside hand because it will encourage the horse to lengthen his whole frame as he stretches his neck into the longer movement. In time, your horse will associate the act of posting with lengthening.

To collect or shorten a horse, you are in effect telling him to carry more of his and your weight on his hindquarters. You do this by closing your lower legs on his sides, tightening your abdominals, pushing your seat bones forward and tilting your pelvis back, sitting deep with a passive hand, and letting the horse's forehand elevate. In order for the croup to come down, the front end must be allowed to come up. Of course this is done in increments using half halts to build the degree of elevation and to slow down the rate of movement by degrees.

One of the simplest ways of introducing collection and speed control is to sit a few strides of trot every now and then so that you can use your legs and seat better to actively drive with a deep seat. It is important to keep your heels down, although I like to think of keeping my knees down, so that my calves can more easily wrap around the horse's sides. Another way to build toward collection is a series of transitions such as trot-walk; walk-trot; trot-halt; halt-trot.

Occasionally you may have to bring a quickly cantering horse down to a trot, walk, halt, and perhaps even a back just to demonstrate your control of him. If this is done tactfully with lightness and the horse *does* respond properly, it can have a very valuable effect on the horse slowing down in the future. Soon he will begin slowing down when he feels your seat asking for collection; the rein aids will need to be minimal. Roughly pulling a horse down to a stop or forcibly backing him is counterproductive and should not be considered a part of horse training.

Square, Straight Halt

As you work toward a more advanced version of the halt, strive for straightness and for the horse to stop with his hind legs under his body and square. You will have better success working on halts if you have first introduced half halts to your horse. A halt should be planned to occur on a straight line after a series of checks. Basically a halt is just a more final, definite half halt. Your seat and weight are your predominant aids for slowing the horse down. Use your lower legs to help drive the horse up to a forward halt. In other words, you don't want the horse to dribble to a stop with one or both hind legs trailing out behind him. You want him to step up crisply and definitely into your hands on the reins. The reins stop the motion of the horse's hind legs. Your legs will also help you to keep the horse straight as he stops. The turn on the forehand and leg-yielding work will pay off here. Your end goal is to have the horse halt so that his hooves describe a perfect rectangle. His front feet should be straight below his front legs, not propped out in front or angled underneath the chest. The hind feet should be below the hocks not out behind them. However, do not fuss and correct the young horse excessively on the straightness or deepness of his halt. Just keep the goals in mind. Rather than looking under the horse's belly to evaluate the stop, have someone on the ground tell you where the legs are positioned and register the feeling in your seat when the horse has stopped square.

Collection

Collection is a state of balanced energy characterized by a dropped croup, engaged hindquarters, flexed abdominals, arched spine, an elevated head and neck, and a flexed poll. The premiere reining horse, as well as the highly schooled dressage horse, exhibits collection. To achieve collection, a horse must be energized, yet restrained. Although advanced collection is way beyond the realm of the young horse, it is the ultimate goal toward which you gradually aim from the first month of riding. Knowing where you are going will help you prevent mistakes along the way that might thwart your horse from attaining collection in the future.

When you were first learning how to ride, your instructor probably told you never to inflict opposing signals on a horse: In crass terms, don't kick and pull at the same time. Yet, as you become more advanced in your skills and your horse becomes physically and mentally ready, you will begin introducing the concept of collection which in essence is the application of seemingly contradictory aids—opposing the forces of your driving to those of the restraining aids.

Here is where optimum intensity and timing become critical because as you begin to practice the concepts of collection, you will find that if a horse is going to become confused, uncooperative, or fractious, it will be when you ask him to accept the confines of collection. Of course, approached properly the lessons of collection should not create a problem. Especially if you follow the cardinal rules of collection: 1. Always collect from back to front, never from front to back. 2. Never create more energy with your legs and seat than you can contain and shape with your hands. If you do, the horse will either push through your aids or feel threatened by their containment and balk or rear.

Relative Straightness

Be careful that you do not try to straighten a young horse too soon. First be sure he is sufficiently forward and on the aids. He must move forward with a regular rhythm and must respond to your aids. The energy from his hindquarters must move directly toward and through his center of gravity up to his neck. Otherwise your straightening efforts can not be effective. However, if a horse is extremely crooked, it would serve no purpose to ride him forward in a crooked fashion for a long period of time because he would develop a harder-to-change muscular tendency. Such a horse would benefit from more extensive work on the longe line with carefully adjusted side reins.

Many horses tend to carry their hindquarters to the right and let their forehands fall to the left. When traveling to the right, the strong left side resists bending to the right and the forehand tends to stay counter-flexed while the hindquarters fall to the inside (right). When traveling to the left the horse will overbend often in the middle of his neck, bulge the right shoulder out, and let the hindquarters swing further off the track to the right. It is difficult for such a horse to hold his head straight on the right rein, he always wants to tip or curl into the left. Such a horse has developed this way of carrying himself so his naturally stronger left hind leg is underneath his body and his weaker right hind leg does not have to do as much work. Therefore you must move his forehand to the right and eventually move the hindquarters to the left so both of his hind legs are under his body.

Crookedness usually appears more exaggerated at the canter and the trot than at the walk. Often a horse's right shoulder will pop out in an avoidance of correct, uniform bending. This is an indication that the neck muscle at the wither attachment needs strengthening. That is why it is so important in early bending exercises to be sure that the horse is bending at the jaw and throatlatch, not in the middle of the neck. Crookedness can also appear as excess curve in a horse's body from his head to his tail or a stiffness in his jaw, poll, neck, back, or croup. If there is stiffness, there can be no supple connection and therefore no natural swing and flexibility to the spine.

Besides feeling how crooked a horse is, it is valuable to view the exact problem on video, in photos, or by watching someone else work the horse.

To counteract the common crookedness as described above, first shorten the reins to a point of contact that the horse accepts without resistance and hold them at that length throughout the straightening. It is helpful to use reins with ridges so that you can gauge whether you have let the reins slip and the horse go back to its crooked way. (Horses can so easily train humans.)

First track left. Sit very evenly on both seat bones. Apply a firm right direct rein, counter-flexing if necessary. This is the main aid to shift the bulging right shoulder to the left so that the points of the shoulders both face straight forward. You may need to weight your right seat bone slightly more. The horse's left shoulder should be held in position with the left leg in front of the girth, if necessary. The right leg can be applied behind the girth to move the hindquarters over to the left so that the right hind leg is relatively straight behind the right front leg. At every moment of compliance, yield so that the horse relaxes into the straightness. Only ask for a few straight steps at a time. Think of straightness as a specific maneuver you are performing such as a leg-yield or a turn on the hindquarters. After a few correct steps, take a break. Never try to hold a horse straight. Develop his straightness.

Now track right. Apply a firm left direct rein. Apply simultaneous right seat bone and right leg behind the girth to initiate a leg-yield configuration. Maintain the boundary of the movement with the left rein. Now add a soft, intermittent right direct rein. At any instance the horse bends to the right (at the jaw and throatlatch) while maintaining body straightness, yield.

Back

Although you may have asked for a few steps of back long before this, you will have better success now since the horse has accepted contact, has been introduced to longitudinal flexion, has learned square halts and is relatively straight. Now backing under saddle will be physically easier for a horse to perform correctly.

The back is a two-beat diagonal gait in reverse (photos 110, 111, and 112). The diagonal pairs should move actively, not reluctantly. From a walk, the horse should be ridden into an energized halt with contact. The transition to back is also a "forward" transition because the horse must be driven up as if he were going to walk. To back from a halt,

110. In preparation for the back, when the young horse first stops he may be slightly above the bit.

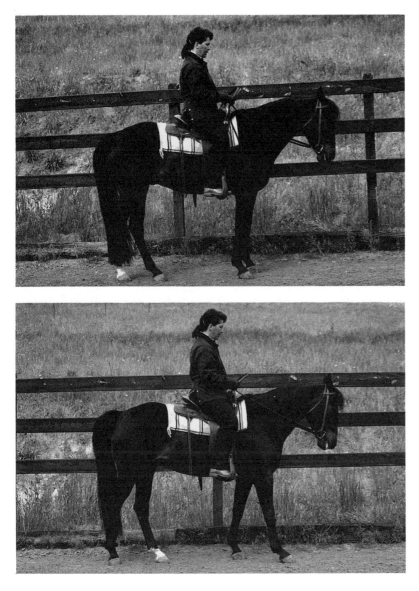

111. Using seat and hands, the horse is softened at the poll and jaw at a standstill.

112. Then with the horse still on the bit, lower leg contact is increased, the reins are shortened slightly, and the horse steps backward with diagonal pairs of legs. Early in backing training, it is natural for a young horse to raise his head when he backs. Later as he develops strength in his back muscles, he will be able to move backward in a longer, lower frame, if desired.

squeeze the horse up to the bit with both legs at the girth. Let him contact the bit and keep your leg pressure on. As soon as you feel the horse begin to round his topline and take the first step back, lighten the rein slightly but keep your legs on. Your horse will likely get even rounder when you lighten rein pressure. Let him take one or two steps back, then let your legs be passive, then drive him forward with your seat into a walk. At first the arena rail will help you keep the horse straight. Ultimately, keep the horse straight by an impeccable balance between your six points of contact: two seat bones, two lower legs, and two hands. Only ask for a few steps of back a couple of times in each training session. It is one maneuver that a horse can get sour on if overworked. Like other new maneuvers, he must develop coordination and strength to perform it for extended periods. Once the horse backs willingly from a halt, work to have him back directly from a walk and then resume walking. Finally, jog, halt momentarily, back, and jog out of the back.

Problems? If a horse locks up when you ask him to back, ride him forward to get him to relax his back again, then ask for a halt and back again. If after about three attempts, he still gets tense, it is probably that he doesn't understand exactly what he should try to do. If you didn't use ground driving as part of his preparatory training, you may need to untrack one of his shoulders at a time to show him what you want. Once you have him driven up to the bit, lightly lift up on one rein as you give with the other and then alternate, letting him wag his body back and forth as he moves backward. Eventually use the previously described standard aids for backing.

THE BALANCE OF THE FIRST YEAR
Introducing the Turn on the Hindquarters

The 360 degree turn on the hindquarters is your eventual goal (photo 113). To get there, first teach your horse to walk around his hindquarters so that his front legs make a bigger circle than his hind legs (Figure 13). If you want him to turn to the left, his right front leg will come close to or cross over and in front of his left front leg. The left front leg takes steps to the inside of the turn. His right hind leg should walk a small circle to the left around his left hind leg which walks an even smaller circle to the left.

To accomplish a rudimentary walk around turn on the hindquarters, first ride a horse in a 66-foot circle and review the previous work with spiraling. Then go back to the large circle and keep a consistent contact on the outside rein so that the horse seems to be making a "straight" circle or almost to the point that at any moment you could counter-flex the horse to the outside of the circle. (Note: This is similar to the beginning stage of the reverse arc training method sometimes used to begin a western horse's spins.) If you are circling left, his head will be looking straight ahead or very slightly to the right. Positioning a horse this way will make it easier for him to keep his weight balanced from left to right as you close up the circle. It will also keep him moving forward, and will set him up to cross his outside front leg over his inside front leg. If you overbend a horse to the inside, he will tend to curl up, lose his forward motion, and it will constrict the movement of his shoulders. Overbending makes it virtually impossible for a horse to cross the outside front leg in front of the inside front leg.

113. The 180° moment of a 360° hindquarter turn to the right. The footfall sequence is the same as the walk: LH, LF, RH, RF. The LH points to the last quadrant of the turn. The LF has crossed over and landed. The RH is swiveling in place and has changed its orientation from pointing left to pointing forward. Next, the RF will uncross and finally the LH (which will then be facing the "old direction" extremely) will lift and orient forward.

114. (above left) Ask for a few steps of a walk-around turn on the hindquarters. Keep the horse's head and neck relatively straight with his weight settled rearward on the inside hind (left hind). And let him walk a portion of a circle. Don't ask for much crossover of the front legs and keep his hindquarters from swinging out of the turn by keeping your outside (right) leg back.

115. (above right) Later, add a small degree of bend to the turn and ask for more of crossover with the front legs. Don't let the horse fall into the turn, however. You might need to hold him up with more outside rein.

Figure 13. Turn on the hindquarters stage 1.

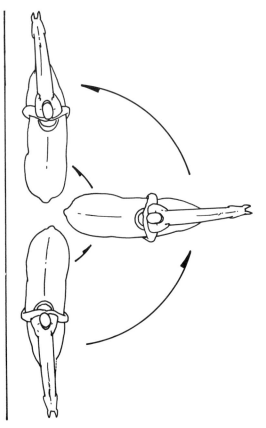

So, with a firm outside rein, apply an active outside leg at the cinch and ask for a few steps to the inside then let your outside leg be passive so the horse can resume his "straight" circle. This is about all that should be expected of a young horse—just that he gets the idea to move his shoulders inward without falling inward (photos 114 and 115). Later, as he gets further along in his training and can hold himself up on the outside rein as well as carry his weight on his inside hind leg, you can ask for a tighter walk around turn on the hindquarters (Figure 14) or pivot (Figure 15). The trainer challenges the young horse for more in photo 113.

Figure 14. Turn on the hindquarters stage 2.

Figure 15. Turn on the hindquarters stage 3.

Neck Reining and the Indirect Rein

If you are training a western horse, once he has learned the leading and direct rein aids thoroughly, you can begin introducing the neck rein. (See Chapter 2 for a discussion of the indirect rein for the procedure to teach the neck rein.)

116. Accustom your young horse to working near other horses.

Riding with Other Horses

As early as is practical (usually by the second month) have another horse and rider work in the arena when you are training (photo 116). It would be best if the other horse was an older, dependable horse such as was described in the ponying section. Plan to regularly work the young horse with another horse in the arena so that you can accomplish the following at all gaits. Ask the rider to follow you around the arena, staying 3 - 4 horse lengths behind, then to pass you with a wide berth and work 3 - 4 lengths in front of you. Once the young horse is accustomed to this, have the rider work alongside you several horse widths away and then on request, either drop behind you or move ahead of you. Then have the rider work in the opposite direction you are working. Finally, ask the rider to stop her horse at various places in the arena so that you can ride past her.

Riding Out and Story Problems

In the arena, your horse learned the equine version of grammar, sentence structure, and the multiplication tables. Now he needs to learn how to put all of that knowledge to use in the real world. As you devise "story problems" for your horse, make them challenging but be sure that everything you ask is fair, safe, and capable of being performed. Facing a horse with an insurmountable task can undermine his confidence for a lifetime; being overly protective of your horse's experiences can make him timid. Therefore, strike a balance.

Once you feel relatively safe riding your young horse in an arena, you should begin riding him out of the arena (photo 117). You might choose to ride out as early as the first month or you may postpone such work

117. As soon as you feel he is ready, begin riding out of the arena to develop a well-rounded young horse.

for several months or more. *When* you ride out is not as important as how successful the experience is. There is no sense losing what you have gained just to say you have ridden out of the arena. When you ride out will depend on your locale, availability of a well-seasoned horse to accompany you, and your skills as a rider. Be sure you have a good base of exercises and responses from your horse so that when you venture out you can use his training to further develop him rather than suffer a setback due to hasty planning. Horses ridden outside of an arena gain valuable experience and a natural type of workout which results in a more confident and well-conditioned athlete. Plan to work your horse once or twice a week outside of the arena.

The first time you ride out, it may be for a few minutes at the end of a lesson. If you have access to a nearby open space such as an uninhabited pasture, cool your horse out by walking on soft rein contact. Over the course of several such rides, familiarize your horse with some of the things he will encounter on the trail rides, road rides, and pasture rides that are in his future.

ROAD RIDING

Riding on a wide shoulder of a safe roadway can provide you with all sorts of opportunities to further your horse's training (photo 118). As you encounter new sights and sounds, you can use them to continue building the horse's confidence. You can capitalize on a horse's reluctance to leave home by working on collected gaits as you head away from home. Conversely use a horse's eagerness to return home to work on lengthening his gaits on the way home. You can use the edge of the road as a guide for your lateral work.

But before a horse can concentrate on performing any specific maneuvers along a road, he must be familiar and relaxed with the surroundings. It is impossible to predict what you will encounter on a road ride, so it will help if you can allow your horse to inspect, ahead of time, the unusual things that are commonly seen along a roadway: culverts and manholes, road signs, pieces of flapping plastic on poles or wire fences, mail boxes, and cattle guards, to mention just a few. You may wish to show him some of these things in-hand first.

When you approach a new object on a ride, proceed at a walk with a relatively soft contact on the reins so that the horse can stretch his neck.

118. Road riding can be a beneficial alternative to arena riding. The first few times at least, ask that a competent horseman on a well-trained, quiet horse accompany you.

This relaxes his back and allows him to reach forward to smell the new object and hopefully allay his fears. Be ready, however, to deal wtih a sudden reaction. If your body language and voice truly convince your horse that there is nothing to fear, he may pass a potentially frightening object with just a sideways glance. If you anticipate a strong reaction to a new object, the horse may sense your apprehension through his back, on his sides, and in his mouth and you may make him unnecessarily suspicious and tense.

It is often beneficial to stage some road-side scenarios so that you can see how your young horse is likely to react. For example, inevitably you will encounter large and noisy vehicles and machinery on a road ride. Tractors, school buses, and road graders tend to overload a horse's sensory apparatus and can cause a horse to panic. Do not expect drivers to be safety conscious or considerate.

Horses that are pastured along side a busy highway may have no fear of large vehicles, but a horse not so broad in his experiences may become terrified if a stock trailer came rattling up behind him or the driver of a large truck applies the air brake just as he passes you. Therefore, familiarize your young horse first with parked cars, pick-up trucks, and tractors, then with vehicles that are idling, and finally with vehicles that are moving. Arrange for someone to repeatedly pass you on the road with a vehicle until your horse is no longer afraid. Initially a horse may veer sideways as the vehicle passes, but by the fourth or fifth pass, his reaction will probably be reduced to just a shudder of concern. It often helps if a horse realizes that there is a human associated with the vehicle. The sound of a human voice allows the horse to relate the vehicle to something he already has experience with and trusts—humans. Exchange verbal greetings with the driver to set a horse at ease. Some horses need further reassurance: Allow the horse to approach the stopped vehicle and smell it or even sniff the driver's outstretched hand.

Although it is generally best not to dismount in order to encourage a horse to move near or over an object, there are no absolutes in horse training. There are occasions where it might be beneficial to lead a horse up to an object. This is where your thorough in-hand work will prove its worth.

Extending the Walk
It is a general recommendation that when you head toward home you work your horse only at a walk for the last mile to prevent the irritating and dangerous habits associated with rushing home to the barn. Capitalize on this time of mandatory walking to work on extending your horse's gait. Extension is characterized by a lengthening and lowering of the horse's frame and stride. It does not constitute an increase in the tempo or speed of a gait. You will not be aiming for an extension such as is pursued in dressage work, but you will want your horse to lengthen and shorten his stride according to your aids. When lengthening, the

rhythm of the horse's steps should remain the same, but he should reach farther forward with each leg.

Because a horse is usually eager to return home, he will be receptive to your leg aids that ask him to reach farther forward with his hind legs. Review the pattern of the walk in your mind: right hind, right front, left hind, left front. That means that just as one particular shoulder is reaching forward and getting ready to land, the opposite hind leg is driving forward. When the right front is settling its weight, the left hind has already landed and is getting ready to push off.

Therefore, the optimum time to cue the horse to move his mass forward with more energy (reach farther underneath himself with his hind legs) is when the diagonal foreleg is off the ground, reaching forward. Weight your left seat bone and apply your left leg in the middle position when the horse's right front leg is reaching forward in order to increase the drive of his left hind leg. Alternating cues between your right and left sides in time with the horse's stride will ask him to step under himself more deeply with both hinds. Normal contact should be maintained through the bridle.

At first the horse may interpret the lengthening aids as a sign to trot, but it doesn't take long to make it clear with your deep seat and steady hands (and perhaps the voice command "walk") that trotting is not wanted. It is tempting to gather up the reins permanently if a horse persists in jogging, but this just compresses him up into a shorter frame, and jogging is about the only way he can dissipate the energy contained in his compacted frame. What you need to do is bring the horse back to a walk by sitting very deep to slow the hind legs and using light intermittent rein pressure to encourage the horse to reach down and slow down. Then ask again with your legs for the extension. The reins must be lengthened somewhat when introducing lengthening. Much later a horse can learn to extend within a shorter rein frame. During an extended walk, you should feel the hips of your horse rocking freely from side to side while the front end exhibits a relaxed rein swinging movement.

Working Along a Road
You can use a road ride as a diversion from the training arena or you can use it in place of an arena lesson. Curves in the road provide an excellent opportunity for you to practice gentle arcing turns. In a continuous arc,

119. Was your
ground training
program sufficient?
You will find out the
first time you
attempt to put on a
slicker while
mounted.

the horse should bend fluidly around your inside leg, inside referring to
the inside of the turn. So, as you ride along a curve to the left, your left
leg is your inside leg. It provides a reference point for your horse which
is especially important when you are way out in the middle of nowhere.
Curves in the road also present a practical reason for you to change
diagonals at the posting trot.

The well-defined edges of a roadway provide a means to measure the
relative straightness of your horse's position and gaits. Making a horse
track perfectly straight ranks as one of the most difficult maneuvers.
Road-side shoulders can also provide a reference for working on leg-
yielding and later, on more advanced lateral work. After a particularly
good session on the road, dismount, loosen the cinch, and lead your
horse the last 1/8 mile home.

MORE STORY PROBLEMS

Slicker: You reviewed sacking out from the ground, now you need to accustom your horse to the sight and sound of you putting on and wearing a slicker while you are mounted (photo 119).

Poles: To create a diversion and to contribute to a horse's coordination, adaptability, flexibility, and muscular development, plan to regularly use ground poles. First lay a single rail on the ground and have the young horse step over it. Place single rails at various places in the arena and around the stable yard. Use squared poles, cavalletti, or railroad ties, not round poles which easily swivel and roll and can cause a horse to panic or trip.

Use a single pole to teach your horse the sidepass. First, walk the horse over the middle of the pole. The next time, stop with his body straddling the pole, his front and hind legs equidistant from the pole. Apply leg-yielding aids intensifying the inside leg and outside rein slightly. You may need to use the outside rein as a quick leading rein to show the horse the way you want him to go (photo 120).

The distance between the poles will depend on a horse's conformation, way of going, gait, and length of stride (photo 121). If your goal is to shorten a horse's stride, move the poles closer together; to lengthen, gradually increase the distance between the poles. The approximate distances given range from those for a very small, short-strided horse to a large, long-strided horse. To teach a horse to pick up his feet and not stumble, use railroad ties, raised poles, or cavelletti.

APPROXIMATE DISTANCE BETWEEN GROUND POLES

	"Stock" Horse	"English" Horse
Walk	1'3" the closest	2'8"
Trot	3' to 3'6"	4'3" to 5'
Canter	6' to 7'	up to 10' 6"

Creek: From the time the horse was a foal, he should have been led through puddles, ditches, and creeks so that when the time comes for him to carry you across water he is not apprehensive. Choose a crossing with safe footing, never one that is dangerously boggy, extremely slippery, rocky, or steep. You might need to allow your horse to lower his head to inspect the water's edge by giving him a long rein and

120. (above left) A single ground pole (or in this case a railroad tie) can act as a guide when teaching the young horse his very first steps of sidepass.

121. (above right) Working a horse over a series of ground poles teaches a horse patience and obedience, can improve his timing and coordination, and adjust the length of his stride.

leaning slightly forward to free his back. However, maintain contact for control and keep both legs on the horse to urge him straight forward. Once all four of his feet are in the water, his head is likely to suddenly come up which, puts slack in the reins. Be ready to gather up the reins to reestablish contact so you can keep him from jumping or rushing. After he has crossed a creek a few times, stop him in the middle of the water and let him relax (photo 122).

Hills, Slopes, and Rocks: A slight upward slope can encourage a horse to use his hindquarters. Going up a hill causes the horse's weight to shift back, requiring him to round his back and reach with his neck in order to flex the hocks and stifles and get up the hill (photo 123). Lean slightly forward to allow the horse's back to work freely.

When traveling downhill, an inexperienced horse can easily become unbalanced and let his weight fall dangerously onto his forehand. Lean slightly back when going downhill to lessen the load on the forehand. (photo 124) Working downhill at a gait other than the walk requires strength, conditioning, and practice for you and your horse. Be sure your horse can walk downhill in a balanced fashion and can work well on the flat at the trot and lope before you attempt to trot or canter downhill.

122. When crossing water, allow your horse to lower his head somewhat to view the water. The young horse that has routinely been walked through water in-hand will find little difficulty negotiating his first creek crossing.

123. Walking across bridges, rock slabs, and concrete require good traction and a calm, cooperative horse.

124. Working on a variety of terrain conditions and helps the young horse to develop balance.

Bridge: If you have led your horse over cement, plywood, and tarps (photo 125), have loaded him into a trailer, and have ridden him over tarps and water, he will have little apprehension about crossing a bridge. Use the same basic procedure as for crossing water.

Gate: Working a gate smoothly and safely from a horse's back is not only handy, but it can be the basis for introducing and then using a good number of maneuvers in concert. Have a plan in mind before you approach a gate and things will go more easily. Since you have already worked a gate in-hand with your horse, riding through should go

125. Walking a horse over a tarp further develops his confidence and adaptability.

smoothly. The in-hand preparation will pay off when it comes time to work a gate from horseback, not because you will use the same sequence of maneuvers, but because the horse has been taught to approach the gate patiently as a formal lesson with a definite plan. There are four ways to properly negotiate a gate from the horse's back. Which one you will use will depend on which way the gate swings, how it hinges, latches, and what types of corners or supports are present near the gate which may inhibit certain positions and sequences.

With a young and inexperienced horse, it is best to take your time with the various components of working the gate so the horse does not become nervous, frightened, or anticipatory. For example, ride up alongside the gate, stand and let the horse relax, and then ride off. The next time, ride up, stand, rattle the gate or latch a bit, stand, and ride off. The horse needs to be comfortable with the workings of a gate so that he will pay more attention to your aids than to the gate itself. Little by little, add the various components described below. Be sure to pause often and add an organized halt in between the segments so the horse does not become anticipatory. The goals for working a gate properly include: Never let go of the gate, do not lose an effective position in the saddle while working the gate, and be able to stop the horse at any moment.

The simplest way to work a gate is to push the gate open and ride forward through it. First, ride alongside the gate and stop with your leg at the latch. Hold the reins in one hand; with the other, unlatch the gate. Then let your hand slide along the top of the gate (photo 126) while you back the horse a few steps so that his head is now at the latch (photo 127). Swing the gate away from the horse so that he sees an inviting opening (photo 128). Later, as the horse progresses, instead of swinging the gate away from the horse, you can have the horse "work the gate" with a few steps of sidepass (similar to a full pass) or turn on the hindquarters. Which one you will use will depend on the length of the gate and how close the horse's haunches must work to the hinges—a very long gate will allow the horse to do more of a sidepass while a short gate will require a few steps of a turn on the hindquarters.

In any case, once the gate is opened, the horse is moved sideways a few steps and walked forward until his shoulder or your leg is at the end of the gate (photo 129). Then perform a turn on the center (photo 130) to position the horse parallel to the opposite side of the gate. In a turn

126. To begin working the gate, stop alongside and unlatch it. Pause. Then with your hand on top of the gate, slide it along as you begin backing your horse.

127. Once your horse's head is in a position to clear the opening, pause momentarily.

128. Swing the gate open and let the young horse look at the opening but make him stand still to prevent future anticipation and rushing through the gate.

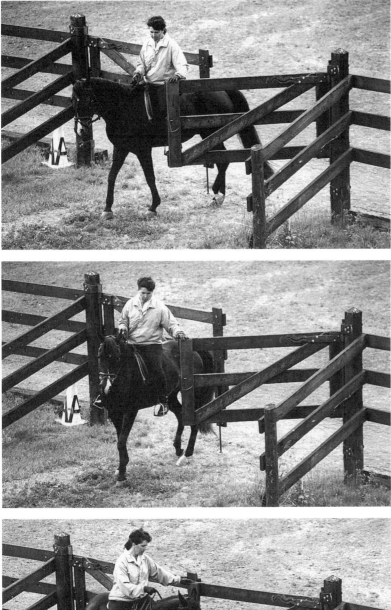

129. Ride the horse forward through the opening. When your leg is at the end of the gate, stop the horse to position him for a turn on the center.

130. Perform a turn on the center (forehand moving to the left, hindquarters moving to the right —a swivel on the middle) until the horse is on the opposite side of the gate.

131. Perform the necessary combination of turn on the hindquarters and sidepass until the gate is closed. Have the horse stand quietly as you latch the gate, then have him stand for a little longer.

on the center, the horse swivels around his middle, his forehand moving left and his hindquarters moving right or vice versa. Then perform as many steps of sidepass or turn on the hindquarters as is required to close the gate (photo 131).

Once the horse has mastered the first way, you can pull the gate toward you to open it and to close it. Although you might think this would be the easier way to first teach the horse because the gate coming toward him would be a visual cue, it seems that more horses get confused or frightened if this method is used first. It seems to be much clearer to a horse initially to ride through an inviting opening. Nevertheless, you should practice pulling the gate toward you because with some gates it will be the only way you will be able to get through.

The third and fourth methods involve backing a horse around the end of the gate. This is often necessary if the latch is located in a tight corner and you cannot reach it by riding forward to it. The way to begin is to position the horse alongside the gate and back him into the corner. Reach back and unlatch the gate and swing it open (or use a few steps of sidepass or turn on the forehand) so that the horse sees and senses that there is an opening he can back through. With the horse's hindquarters positioned in the opening, back the horse a few steps so that your leg is at the end of the gate. Then perform a turn on the center where the hindquarters rotate through the gate opening followed by the forehand. Once the horse's body is parallel to the gate, but now on the back side, a few steps of sidepass will close the gate so you can latch it.

The fourth method is for a latch in a corner and especially one with a restricted area inside the gate. Here the gate is opened toward the horse and utilizes a combination of turn on the center and rein back as the horse works around the end of the gate. This last method would be the most difficult to start with but presents no big problem if the horse has been taught the other methods first.

7

Physical Evaluation and Development

Conformation Evaluation

Many factors contribute to a horse's individual athletic ability, one of the greatest being the horse's conformation. However, a young horse's conformation may or may not be a true indication of what he will be like as an adult. When experienced horsemen are asked at what age the young horse gives the best indication of what his conformation will be like as an adult, the replies vary greatly. Some say you never know until the horse matures while others use a specific age such as two days, weaning, or the beginning of the two-year-old year to make a prediction. Many feel that the period from weaning through the yearling year is an inconsistent and awkward phase especially in terms of balance, angles, and proportions. As the mounted training program begins, objectively evaluate your young horse. It will prove helpful in designing his custom exercise program as well as understanding his physical abilities and limitations. A conformation analysis should include an evaluation for quality, substance, proper proportions and correct angles.

Quality is the overall merit of the horse, largely determined by genetics and exemplified by well-defined features, smooth hair coat and classy appearance. Head, throatlatch, and joints are clean, not heavy or meaty. The tongue should be soft and thin-skinned, not coarse or tough. Look at the interdental space and note the thickness of the jawbone and the quality of the skin covering it.

Substance refers to height and weight, depth and type of muscling, circumference and density of bone, roominess of joints, and size of hooves. It is not important to actually measure the circumference of cannon bones in order to assess substance. What is important is that the substance is balanced throughout the horse; that the bones, joints, and hooves are an appropriate size to support the body. A horse can exhibit both quality and substance.

Proportions dictate how well the horse's body will work as a unit. Young horses often do not seem to have ideal proportions but frequently grow into themselves. The adult should have an approximately equal relationship between leg length and depth of girth, but the young horse is almost always longer of leg. The forehand should not be more heavily muscled than the hindquarters and in this regard young horses are often balanced. The adult topline should conform to these ratios: the neck should be equal to or greater in length than the back and the rump should be equal to or greater than two-thirds the length of the back. Often very young horses have shorter necks and the croup is often higher than the withers.

Correctness of *angles,* particularly of the limbs, gives a horse a better chance of reaching his performance potential while remaining sound. New-born foals may appear to have very sloping shoulders and pasterns and a very steep croup and over-angulated hind legs due to muscle laxity. Within a few days, provided the foal receives normal exercise, the limbs will attain a more normal configuration. Due to rapid growth, the weanling and yearling sometimes appear steeper in the limbs than they will as adults.

Although the textbook descriptions of "ideal" horse conformation are relatively standard, we have all seen exceptions to the rules. We have seen horses with short, thick necks out handle the clean-cut, long and shapely-necked horse; we've seen sickle-hocked, curby horses use their hind ends in a way that puts the horse with ideal hind legs to shame; we've seen horses with backs long enough for the whole family somehow get organized into a balanced and attractive package when they move. However, in general, certain conformational traits tend to be associated with certain types of movement.

I know what it is like to ride a steep-shouldered, short-pasterned, ground pounder, a big, heavy horse, or a beefy, lumbering, downhill individual. I have also been on slab-sided, narrow-chested, weak-backed, and rubbery individuals. So when I am evaluating a young horse, I look at him wondering what he will feel like when I put my saddle on him in the future. I look for a fluid, graceful horse that moves more like a dancer than a weight lifter. I don't place a heavy emphasis on muscle mass because excess muscle is not required for a riding horse. On the other hand, an excessively willowy animal may not have the strength necessary to do the work I require. I look for moderate muscles that are long and stretchy and tie low into the knees and hocks.

Movement. I note any deviations in travel that may cause interference or performance problems. Although it is true that there have been great horses that wing in or paddle, such movement signifies inefficient and possibly dangerous movement. I like to see a horse trot past me in a straight line so I can assess his movement from the side. I look at the length and slope to his shoulder and see whether the horse can move his shoulder in a forward, flowing motion. There should be no exaggerated knee flexion. The horse should land softly and lightly. If I hear or see a horse pounding, I think he will be hard on my back and his legs.

I like the hind feet of a western horse to track up and meet or land on top of the imprints from the front feet. This tells me the horse is capable of using his back and his hindquarters in a way that allows his hind legs to work well under his belly. I like a western pleasure-type horse to hold his hind legs rather straight in the hock as he swings them underneath himself. This tells me he has a relaxed, elastic back that bows upward as his hind legs come forward. For a more active western horse (ranch work, reining, etc.) a little more hock action is appropriate for the increased activity of the work, but I still do not want to see a lot of hock flexion or snap.

If I am looking at a dressage prospect, I want his hind feet to step ahead of his front prints. And I look for more flexion of the hock because (provided the back is working correctly) this will tell me the horse will have an easier time with the more collected movements. Depending on the individual style of a dressage prospect's movement, there may or may not be more knee flexion.

Balance. Balance makes it easier for some horses to perform than others. Although a downhill horse (one who is lower at the withers than the hip) *might* be able to move in a balanced fashion, it will usually be much more difficult for him than a horse whose withers are equal to or higher than his croup. A downhill horse will have difficulty shifting his weight to the hindquarters and carrying it, especially if the imbalance is coupled with a flat croup. Young horses often go through growth spurts which cause them to travel heavy on the forehand, be strung out behind, and may cause them to forge. A downhill horse needs to be ridden with a solid connection each day for as long a period of time as the horse's condition level can maintain a correct frame. This will strengthen his topline and prepare him for rebalancing which will come later.

I take the growth spurts of yearlings (which result in an uneven topline) into consideration, but I'm skeptical of two-year-olds and especially three-year-olds that show extreme variations between the height of the withers and croup. But even if a horse's topline is level, if he has an excessively heavily muscled forehand in comparison to his hindquarters, he is going to have difficulty flowing forward freely.

Neck. I avoid a horse with a ewe neck, one that is flat or concave on the top with a bulge underneath. With this kind of neck, the horse's head is held up by a contraction of the under neck muscles, therefore those muscles have become very strong and prominent. This is a self-perpetuating configuration. In order to achieve connection and balance, the top neck muscles must be stretched and strengthened and the lower muscles must be allowed to quit working and relax. This is very difficult and requires a lot of correct work in a long, low frame such as the use of side reins with longeing or the rider using very low hands. Cavalletti work may also be helpful.

A swan neck joins the withers at a relatively high point and has an exaggerated bend at the poll. Usually the neck is long and thin and often wobbly, breaking under pressure at the withers. Such a horse should be ridden forward and low for a long time to develop the strength (of the muscles just in front of the withers) and the reach necessary before a shorter connection is attempted.

Back. I like a horse's back to have a naturally inviting place to put a saddle. This begins with prominent withers that reach to behind the heart girth and blend gradually into the back—this will indicate that the horse has a sloping shoulder. I do not like meaty, short withers located far forward as they are usually accompanied by a straight shoulder and are associated with saddle slippage.

The muscles that run alongside both sides of the spine should tend to be flat rather than sloped—the back should look like a place to play checkers rather than a place to ski. Flat, strong back muscling (fit, not fat) ensures the bearing surface of the saddle will be properly supported, which will minimize back problems.

A short back is usually a strong back and makes a horse relatively easy to collect because the hind legs can step well under the horse's center of gravity. However, some short-backed horses tend to be short-strided or when moving out will forge (slap the toe of the hind foot with the bottom of the front foot on the same side usually during a trot). Work must focus on suppling and stretching (lengthening) to develop the horse's maximum potential. If a short-backed horse has a long neck and a long hip, there is often no problem. A combination of a short neck, short croup, and short back, however, can result in a stiff horse which can be uncomfortable to ride.

A long back may be a dividend or a detriment. At first a long-backed horse may be more difficult to put to the aids, but once accomplished he will be able to flex and swing his back and be more comfortable to ride. If a long-backed horse has adequate muscling in the back and loin, there should be no problem. If, however, a horse has back muscles that are weak or slope away from the vertebrae, he will have more of a tendency to develop a sore back and may need to be worked extensively on the longe with side reins to develop these muscles. A *very* long-backed horse may have difficulty stepping up underneath his center of gravity for the collected work especially if his extremely long back is coupled with being camped out behind (straight hind legs).

The loin should be well-muscled and relatively short. I strongly discredit a horse with a weak and/or long loin and coupling, as this type of horse is notorious for hollowing his back. A horse that chronically hollows his back is setting the stage for problems with pinched nerves or vertebrae damage. Such a horse is often difficult to organize and collect and can give the rider the impression that she is riding two separate horses. The loin and the coupling are what tie the motion of the hindquarters to the front end, so they must be strong and well, connected.

A horse with a flat croup is at a disadvantage for collected work but should do well in extended work. Such is the anatomical feature that makes many purebred and part-bred Arabian horses excel at long distance riding and many Quarter Horses excel at work on the hind-quarters.

I prefer a horse with a deep heart girth and some spring to its ribs. Besides providing room for the heart, lungs, and digestive tract, a horse with moderate curvature to its ribs provides a natural, comfortable place for a rider's legs. A slab-sided horse with a shallow heart girth is tough to ride properly because it is difficult to cue the horse effectively with the legs. A horse with a very round barrel is uncomfortable to ride as the shape of his ribs tends to cause a rider's legs to spread excessively and take on an A-frame configuration.

The horse's leg length (chest floor to ground) should be about equal to the distance from the chest floor to the top of the withers. Legs shorter than this and the horse would be more like a sewing machine and less like the dancer or gymnast I am looking for.

Hind legs. Because one of the main goals of a horse's physical development is that he accepts more weight with the hindquarters, it is imperative that he have correct hind leg conformation. A horse with more "set to his hocks," often called sickle-hocked, may be able to step underneath himself due to the advantage provided by his overangulated hocks; however, his predisposition to hock lamenesses is high. Crooked hocks and fetlocks may cause problems when a horse is asked to increase the flexion of the joints and carry more weight with the hind legs.

Muscles. A horse with the proper length, proportions, and angles to his skeleton and moderate muscling to tie it all together will have an easier time performing in most of today's performance events. I avoid the horses with short, thick muscles or flat, willowy muscles. One of the best places to evaluate the depth and length of a horse's muscle is the forearm and chest. The muscles running along the inside and outside of the forearm should go all the way to the knee, ending in a gradual taper, rather than ending abruptly a few inches above the knee. This will allow the horse to use its front legs in a smooth, sweeping, forward motion. The pectoral muscles at the horse's chest floor, often referred to as the inverted V, should also reach far down. These muscles help a horse move its legs sideways. The horse with a flat-floored chest may have trouble performing lateral movements.

I like a horse with an attractive head, but I look more for an honest, sensible eye, an alert, tractable expression to the ears, and proper chewing and breathing apparatus than I do for a doll head. If a horse has a tiny, trim head but an expression in the eyes and ears that says "Stay away," I do just that. Training will come easier for a young horse that has sound, functional conformation.

OTHER PHYSICAL TRAITS

Besides conformation, other physical traits need to be considered. Observing young horses at play in a pasture can separate those with the natural propensity for dressage from those that would excel at jumping; those that show the smooth gaits for western pleasure and those that show the athletic ability for reining maneuvers. If you are looking for a western riding or reining prospect or a dressage prospect, watch for individuals that carry their weight rearward and that are naturally supple to both the right and left—those horses that bend easily in the direction of movement no matter which lead they are on and that perform natural, fluid lead changes. Some other movement-related factors that can be assessed are natural carriage and topline, length of stride, physical sensitivity and responsiveness, reflexes, and coordination.

The proprioceptive sense allows a horse to rely on neuromuscular transmissions rather than entirely on sight to negotiate an obstacle. This is essential for trail horses, hunter/jumpers, and eventers. There are many simple things that can be done to demonstrate a young horse's kinesthetic abilities. Very young horses can be led over ground rails which are about 5 feet apart. Compare the first, second and third passes over the rails. If the horse maintained composure all three times, pay special attention to him. If he does well the first time but his performance deteriorates, it may indicate the pattern of his future work, that he pays attention to what is new and then becomes easily bored. If a horse taps a rail on the initial pass but improves on the successive attempts, he shows good learning potential.

The horse's ability to balance his shifting weight, and later the rider's, during various maneuvers, is necessary in all sports. Remember, equilibrium is measured from side to side as well as from front to rear. Some horses have lateral balance problems. If a horse longes in a smooth arc with freedom of movement in one direction but stiffly and awkwardly in the other, he is not naturally balanced laterally. Horses that routinely take the counter lead or canter disunited when longed in a 20-meter circle have inherent balance problems.

The flexibility of the horse's spine is especially important for dressage, jumping, and reining. A horse that consistently carries its head and neck away from the direction of travel is stiff and resistant in his body. A stiff horse can experience pain and/or damage when he is required to bend. A horse should be able to arc his head around to each shoulder without distress and without moving his hindquarters. Holding a horse along a solid fence and trying this on each side will reveal muscular resistance.

To see how handy a horse is at settling his weight on the hindquarters and changing direction, you can step in front of the horse while he is trotting or loping in a round pen. These gaits have the impulsion necessary for the average horse to do a rollback into the fence. Watch for the horse that drops his croup, raises his head, makes a clean, 180-degree sweep, and comes out on the opposite lead. A young horse that can perform a clean pivot over the hocks at a walk shows a great degree of natural talent, strength, and balance. As a horse loads in a trailer, he experiences a weight shift to his hindquarters and then to his forehand. This should happen smoothly and without exaggerated head and neck movements or a clumsy use of the hindquarters.

If looking for an English prospect, ground rails can help evaluate the horse's stride. The yearling can be longed at the trot over rails to assess its honesty, cooperation, and coordination. A small fence can be added at the end of the ground rails for the hunter prospect. Natural jumping talent and balance show up as the horse goes over a fence the first time. Subsequent attempts might show that the horse retains an interest or that he is getting careless or bored.

Coordination is closely coupled to the proprioceptive sense. A horse is well-coordinated if his body functions harmoniously when performing complex movements. Ask a yearling to canter just as he approaches a 1-foot jump in his longeing pen. Watch the way a prospect changes leads as he plays in the pasture.

A sensitive horse will be more receptive to aids. Individuals with large eyes and nostrils and keen hearing perceive more subtle distinctions in their environment. Nerve endings on the thin-skinned, sensitive horse are close to the surface and readily receive stimuli from the rider's aids. Approach a group of horses in a pasture. Which one is the first to hear you as you approach?

You already have a good idea of your horse's sensitivity to pressure on his ribs from moving him over while he was tied. To further check his reflex reactions, exert pressure on his tendon above the fetlock. What is necessary to get the horse to pick up his hoof? Examine his tongue. Is it pink, soft and thin-skinned or meaty and tough? Look inside his mouth at the interdental space. Is the skin covering the lower jaw heavy or thin?

The ratio of fat to muscle in the growing horse should be very low. A young horse that is an easy keeper, or has larger fat stores than his herd mates, may have a lower metabolic rate and/or a more efficient digestive system. Although this may seem to be an advantage from a management standpoint, an overweight youngster may be prone to bone or joint problems. A young horse that has the tendency to deposit fat in the neck or over the croup, may have difficulty as an adult with freedom of movement in those areas.

Tough joints and elastic, but durable tendons are necessary for any performance, especially those on deep, hard or irregular surfaces.

Watch a prospect play in a deep sand pen, in a paddock with a hard surface, and in a pasture with uneven terrain. In each case, watch the flexion and extension of the joints and the horse's overall freedom of stride and compensatory head and neck movements. The horse that has an easy time on all three footings probably has the legs for nearly any performance event. Short, steep pasterns flex very little causing the joints to bear considerable concussion and creating a stiff ride. Long, sloping pasterns can either provide a more comfortable or a more bouncy ride and can lead to stressed tendons and joints.

The efficiency of the heart and lungs in providing oxygen and dispersing waste products during and after exercise changes dramatically as the horse matures. Rapid breathing and heart rate are characteristic of the young horse. While normal resting adult pulse rates vary between 35 and 40 beats per minute, normal resting rates for the yearling are 45 to 60 and for the two-year-old 40 to 50 beats per minute. Normal resting respiration rates range from about 12 to 25 breaths per minute with young horses at the high end of the scale. If a prospect is destined for endurance or race-related events, comparison of pulse and respiration with herd mates may be valuable. The rate of recovery after exertion is most important. Two-year-olds that don't respond to conditioning programs may be inappropriate candidates for such events.

Physical relaxation is necessary for maximum athletic achievement. A horse that is not capable of releasing tension is working against himself during performance. Muscles are essentially involved in a give-and-take situation as they contract and relax. If a horse cannot relax as he is working, he is creating a drag on one of his muscle groups because the reciprocal group cannot adequately release its tension. That's why it is essential to choose a young horse with the length and depth of muscling for the proposed event.

Strength, which is an all-out effort exerted by a single contraction of a muscle, is necessary for explosive sports such as roping, so the roping horse needs thick, dense muscles. At the other end of the spectrum is the endurance horse which requires stamina, not speed, so must have long, thin muscles that can withstand repeated contractions. Choose a young horse with the depth of muscle appropriate for your activity.

Horses must breathe regularly throughout a workout and need to be relaxed in order to establish a rhythm. Watch a young horse in training on the longe line when he is asked to stop, to collect or extend a gait; look for signs of tension when there is pressure exerted on the bit during ground driving. Watch if the horse tends to hold his breath and then gasp for air or if he strikes up a breathing rhythm appropriate for his work. This is especially critical for horses chosen for racing, gymkhana, endurance, and eventing.

Physical Development

Teaching a young horse *what* to do is only part of the training equation. When you teach him *how* to do things, you begin developing his body so that he will be able to perform in a correct form more easily. In order to do this you must understand the overall goals, assess your horse's tendencies, understand principles of balance and movement, and formulate a plan appropriate for his conformation and your goals.

GOALS
* Gradually change the horse's flat or hollow topline to a bowed topline.
* Develop suppleness and strength evenly on both sides of the body.
* Gradually shift the weight of the horse from the forehand to the hindquarters.
* Improve the style or expression of the horse's movement.
* Improve the quality of the gaits.

To add to the conclusions you made when you evaluated your horse according to the preceding guidelines, perform the following simple tests. Note the horse's behavior in each direction. Did he stop, throw up his head, balk, swerve, push his shoulder into you, fall on his forehand, swing his hindquarters off to the side, trip, fall, rear?

TEST BATTERY TO REVEAL PHYSICAL TENDENCIES
Lead horse in both direction from both sides
Turn horse both ways from both sides
Lead over ground rails
Longe over ground rails at the trot
Longe at trot and canter on a 30-foot line both ways
Longe at trot and canter on 10 to 15-foot line both ways
Evaluate lead problems
Longe over small jump
Free longe and ask horse to roll back into the fence at the
     lope and lope off in the opposite direction
Compare sensitivity of ribs by moving horse over both
     ways

Understanding Anatomy and Movement

To add to the conclusions you've drawn from an external conformation evaluation of your horse, assess his structure and movement anatomically to form a complete picture.

THE SPINAL COLUMN
Refer to Figure 16 for the location of all of the subsequent
     terms.

7 cervical vertebrae	C 1-7	neck
18-19 thoracic vertebrae	T 1-18 or 19	back
5-6 lumbar vertebrae	L 1-5 or 6	loin
5 sacral vertebrae (fused)		croup
18 coccygeal vertebrae		tail

The neck. The first cervical vertebrae, the atlas, has a generous opening where the enlarged spinal cord passes on its way to join the brain. The atlas has large flat wings on either side, which can be felt just behind the ears of your horse at the poll. These broad surfaces allow for attachment of neck muscles and ligaments. The joint between the atlas and the skull allows for flexion and extension. The second cervical

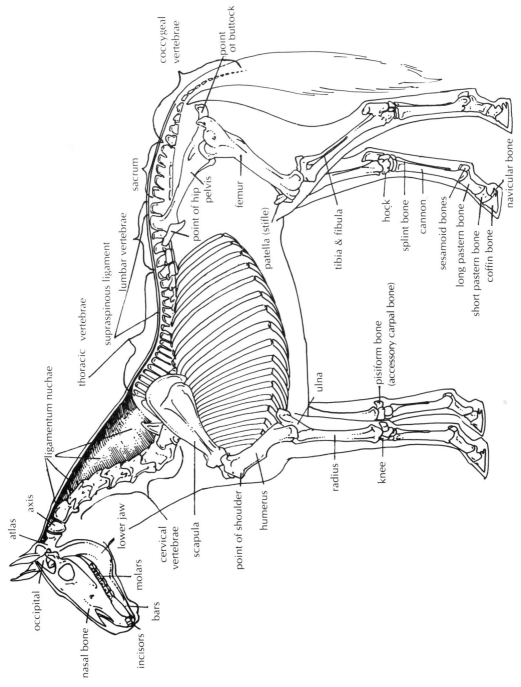

Figure 16. Skeleton.

vertebrae, the axis, has a very large central spine along its top for attachment of neck muscles and ligaments, especially the ligamentum nuchae. The joint between the atlas and the axis allows for sideways (lateral) movement as well as flexion and extension. Cervical vertebrae three through seven allow for both lateral movement and flexion and extension. A horse that gets behind the bit often overflexes by rounding his neck at the third and fourth cervical vertebrae to avoid contact with the bit.

The ligamentum nuchae is a very thick, strong elastic ligament which runs from the poll to the withers and joins with the supraspinous ligament of the back, so in effect, ties the whole spine of the horse together from the poll to the tail. The ligamentum nuchae supports the head and neck. Therefore when a horse stretches forward and down, the ligamentum nuchae via the supraspinous ligament brings the back up. When a horse shortens his topline by raising the neck and hollowing the back, the ligaments go slack so are ineffective. The ligaments must be strengthened by progressive training in order to help hold the back up for hind leg flexion.

The back. Each of the thoracic vertebrae has a rib. T 3 - 10 make up the withers with number 7 the point at which a horse's height measurement is taken. The front leg should be positioned below T 4. The spines of the thoracic vertebrae face toward the back of the horse.

The loin. Most horses have six lumbar vertebrae. Some Arabians have only five and may have an extra thoracic vertebrae. Generally the lumbar vertebrae fuse, often as early as two years of age. When fusion takes place on one side and not the other, it could cause the horse to travel crooked or feel pain. The spines of the lumbar vertebrae face the front of the horse.

The croup. The sacrum is essentially five vertebrae fused into one solid mass. This creates a structure strong enough to receive and transmit the thrust from the hind legs. The junction of the lumbar vertebrae and the sacrum is the point where flexion of the croup takes place.

The tail. The (approximately) eighteen coccygeal vertebrae make up the tail.

Center of Gravity
The terms *center of gravity, center of balance,* and *center of mass* are all relatively synonymous and refer to a theoretical point in the horse's

body around which the mass of the horse is equally distributed. At a standstill, the center of gravity is the point of intersection of a vertical line dropped from the highest point of the withers and a line from the point of the shoulder to the point of the buttock (Figure 17). This usually is a spot just behind the elbow and two-thirds of the distance down from the topline of the back.

Although the center of gravity remains relatively constant when a highly trained and conditioned horse moves, young horses rebalance their weight (and that of the rider and tack) with every stride to counteract the forces of gravity. In order to simply pick up a front foot to step forward, a horse must shift his weight rearward. How much the weight shifts to the hindquarters depends on the horse's conformation, the position of the rider, the gait, the degree of collection, and the goals of the performance.

As a horse collects, the hindquarters, which are normally a driving force, will also become somewhat more of a carrying or supporting factor. The more collected a horse moves, the more his hindquarters are set under his body (engaged), the more he flexes his abdominals, the more he rounds his spine from poll to tail, and the more elevated his head and neck become. In the highly collected dressage horse or the stopping reiner, the horse rocks his weight onto the hindquarters and

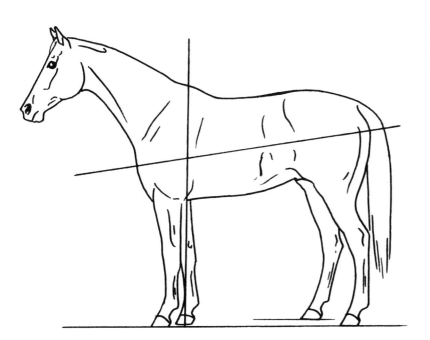

Figure 17. Center of gravity (K. D. Blackwell)

places his hind legs deep under his belly close to his center of gravity.

The degree of collection appropriate for a young horse is a matter of opinion. Because of the slow, relaxed gaits often characteristic of a young horse, he does not need to shift his weight nearly as far back as the horse performing a piaffe or sliding stop. But if you are looking toward the future, you want the young horse to begin using his hindquarters as soon as he is able. A horse that drives from behind when he is quietly loping will likely be able to stop naturally in balance, get over a fence, or switch leads naturally when the time comes.

Yet with many young horses, the hindquarters are not carrying their own weight, let alone some of the displaced weight from the forehand, barrel, or that of the saddle and rider. Instead, all of that weight is being sent in a downward direction to the forehand which makes it even more difficult for the front end to efficiently handle the power and movement sent from the hindquarters. In order to get out of the way of the energy sent from behind, the horse has to lift his forehand up *before* moving it forward. This is done by snapping or flexing the knee joint in order to clear the ground and results in a less comfortable ride as well as being energy inefficient and mechanically unsound. The naturally balanced horse simply has an easier time getting out of his own way than the unbalanced horse.

Movement

A horse needs to be able to move freely in order to move forward in balance. He must be able to utilize (in varying degrees according to his physical development and conditioning) the upswing and downswing of his neck and croup, especially at the canter, in order to make the system of muscular and skeletal components work. For example, the downswing of the front end pulls the back up with the help of the trapezius, longissimus dorsi, and spinalis dorsi muscles and the ligamentum nuchae. If the young horse is prevented from reaching down he will develop a hollow back. If a horse is prevented from raising his head up during the upswing phase of the canter, he will not be able to get his hindquarters underneath himself. The trainer must discover the balance point of each untrained horse and gradually develop it.

Knowing some facts about front leg movement is also helpful. As the trapezius and rhomboideus muscles contract, they lift a front foot. These muscles act best when the neck is optimally arched. If the head and neck are too low it is too much work for the muscles to lift the leg. If the head is too high and overbent, there is a limited amount of additional action that can be created by the contraction of these muscles. The brachiocephalic muscle pulls the front leg forward and is most efficient if the horse's neck is extended out in front of the horse's shoulder. If the neck is too high and pulled back, it will cause the front leg to snap up as well as forward. Horses that pull themselves forward using their front leg muscles, instead of driving from behind and using their neck and shoulder muscles, will often develop large forearm and pectoral muscles.

Muscle contraction is only one side of the coin; the other side is a blend of muscle relaxation and optimal resistance. Think of movement as a series of give-and-take situations. Agonist muscle groups initiate a particular movement at the same time antagonist muscles allow, yet slightly resist that movement. For example, the flexor muscles at the back of the forearm can act as an agonist and "take" as they contract and flex the knee and lift the front leg into the air; meanwhile the extensors at the front of the forearm give to allow the flexors to work, yet the extensors provide enough resistance so the resulting movement is stable and smooth, not wobbly. Then when the extensor muscles at the front of the forearm act as agonists and contract to extend the limb, the forearm flexors take the role as antagonists and give while providing a necessary measure of resistance. Antagonists stabilize joint movement and help to protect joints against overflexion or hyperextension.

Cooperative antagonism is based on the intrinsic ability of the horse to relax particular muscles in order to allow other muscles to establish supremacy. This results in ease of contraction for the agonist while still providing sufficient resistance to prevent dislocations, sprains, and ligament tears. Some horses have a much more highly developed innate synchronization of their agonist and antagonist groups. Others may experience excess drag from certain antagonist groups (in the form of tension) making the agonist muscles work unnecessarily hard. Still others, notably young or under-conditioned horses, may be unable to provide sufficient resistance with certain antagonists, resulting in weak, wobbly, asymmetric or otherwise unbalanced movements.

Hind leg movement depends on the flexion of the hip joint, the stifle, and the hock in order for the leg to move forward. During forward movement, as the horse's hind foot reaches ahead, the lumbo-sacral

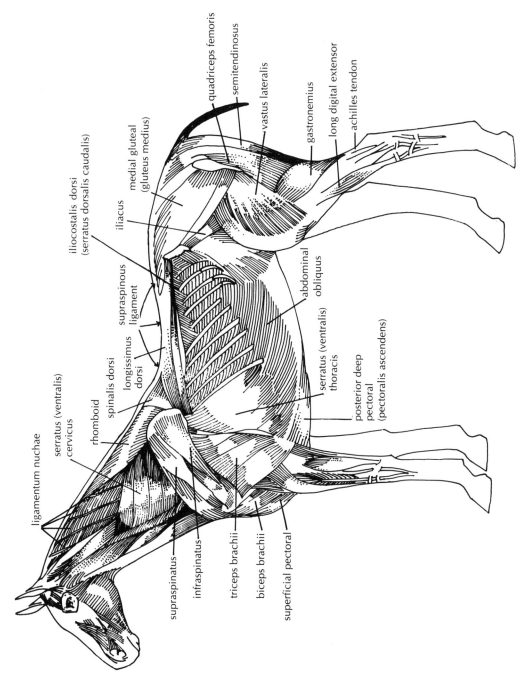

Figure 18. Deep muscles.

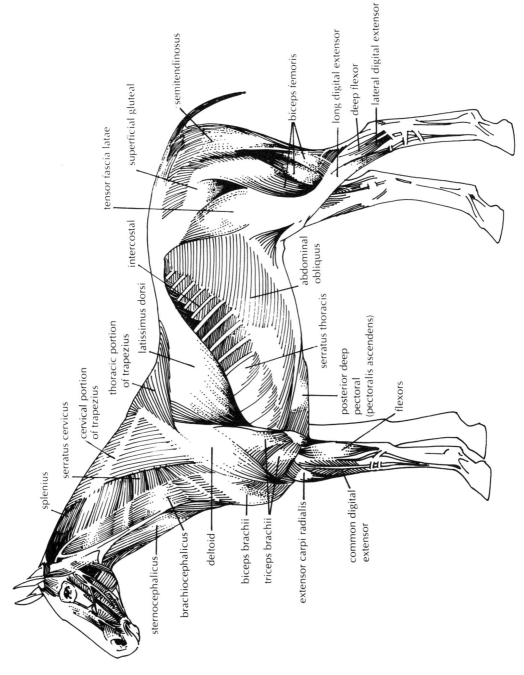

Figure 19. Superficial muscles.

splenius

serratus cervicus

cervical portion
of trapezius

thoracic portion
of trapezius

latissimus dorsi

intercostal

tensor fascia latae

superficial gluteal

semitendinosus

biceps femoris

long digital extensor

deep flexor

lateral digital extensor

abdominal
obliquus

serratus thoracis

posterior deep
pectoral
(pectoralis ascendens)

flexors

sternocephalicus

brachiocephalicus

deltoid

biceps brachii

triceps brachii

extensor carpi radialis

common digital
extensor

joint flexes and the sacrum moves down and forward. The pelvis rotates down and forward by the contraction of the abdominals and is stabilized by the resistance from the longissimus dorsi. A dropped croup (well-engaged hindquarters) is a misnomer as it is actually the flexion of the hip (coxofemoral) joint which rotates the pelvis and produces engagement. The horse's back is stretched between the elastic tension of the croup and buttock muscles (which exert a strong pull down and backward on the muscles of the back) and the elastic tension of the ligamentum nuchae caused by the extension of the head and neck forward. This makes it possible for the head and neck to act as a lever on the hindquarters.

During the walk and trot, the hind legs work independently; one moves forward while the other moves backward. In canter, on the other hand, both hind legs move forward (although one is slightly ahead of the other) at the same time resulting in lumbo-sacral flexion (a hinging downward and forward of the hindquarters, which takes place at the loin).

As each limb pushes off, it needs a rigid structure against which to push. As a foreleg pushes off, the spinalis dorsi contracts and provides the necessary positive resistance; with a hind leg, the longissimus dorsi contracts to provide rigidity. These contractions lift the vertebrae (slightly arch the back) and hold the back rigid. If a horse is holding its head and neck high, inverted, or has a hollow back and/or a flat croup, these muscles have a difficult time contracting effectively.

Even though a horse should move easily and fluidly, a certain amount of positive resistance is necessary between horse and rider (photo 132). Positive resistance should be thought of as muscle tone, not tension and certainly not unwillingness. But just like in dancing, it is easier to lead and follow if there is a bit of positive resistance between partners. A good rider feels the horse and his movement through his seat, legs, and hands and is able to communicate to the horse through subtle body movements. Although you should feel the energy of the horse in his body and via the bridle, the energy should never take the form of tension. Tension is counterproductive resistance and shows either a lack of talent or training in the horse or rider. *Positive* resistance is optimal contact that allows you to feel the horse and ultimately to shape him.

The energy that originates from the hindquarters should be trans-

132. A certain amount of "positive resistance" or contact is necessary between horse and rider and will vary according to your style of riding.

ferred to the front end in an efficient manner. The shortest distance from point A to point B is a straight line. Legs that move straight forward with no inward or outward deviations, no rolling of hocks, no excess flexion or snap, are efficient.

The horse that uses his hind legs relatively straight forward, with very little rotational motion and with minimal flexion, will usually use his back in a springy fashion. The horse that rolls or snaps his hocks excessively is often compensating for a rigid or hollow back. The horse with a sore back will often jerk his hocks up and put them down rapidly rather than reaching his hind legs forward in an unhurried, long, relaxed stride. Usually a horse that uses his hind legs efficiently will be correspondingly efficient with his front end and will, as a result, be a smooth mover.

Unless specifically desired because of breed or type, the front legs should exhibit minimal flexion of the knee joint (the "flat knee") and no inward or outward deviation. The shoulder gives the front legs their angle of efficiency. If a horse has a very steep shoulder, when he sets his foot out, it is not going to end up very far in front of his body; his reach will be rather limited, stabby. However, a horse with a long, sloping shoulder can really reach forward and lay that leg out in front of his body with a ground-covering stride.

In a forward striding horse, the hoof will land flat or slightly heel first which contributes to the forward rolling motion of the horse. A horse that "tippy-toes" lands toe first, stabbing at the ground. This has the effect of breaking the continuity of the gait because the horse is, in effect, on the verge of stopping with each step. He may land abruptly or drag his toes, tending to cause him to trip or stumble.

Center of Rotation

Two areas of the top line are particularly crucial to the uninterrupted flow of muscular activity: The loin, the igniter of propulsive power, is the point of rotation for the movement created by the forelegs and neck. The base of the neck, the transformer of energy, is the point of rotation for the movement created by the hindquarters.

The horse basically pushes himself forward by using his loin, hips, and hocks. So that the hind legs can swing underneath the horse's barrel, the loin must be "well-hinged," that is, strong, yet flexible. The loin (lumbo-sacral joint) has the ability to round upward or to hollow downward. If the forehand is moving properly and the loin is supple and rolling, the horse's back will flex and extend with each stride. If the forehand is out of balance, it makes it almost impossible for the loin to move in the desirable wave-like manner. Instead, short circuits or glitches begin appearing all along the horse's spine, which result in decreased smoothness of movement.

The propulsion that is generated by the hindquarters must be transmitted forward at the same time that the horse bends the spine to accept greater loads with the hind legs. The loin must be relaxed to allow a downward swing of the lumbosacral joint, so important to forward movement.

At the neck, flexor and extensor energy is integrated. When the energy that is created by the hindquarters is sent up to the forehand of the balanced horse, it travels an upward path toward the neck vertebrae located just in front of the withers. The "reaching outward and upward" of the extensors is coupled with the "downward compression" of the flexors and the result is forward movement. Here is another place in the horse's spine where a considerable range of motion is possible: besides moving to either side, the horse can flex and round his neck upward or tense and hollow the neck downward.

Although a neck should be long and supple, a neck can be too long. Trying to turn a horse with a long, thin, wobbly and rubbery neck is like

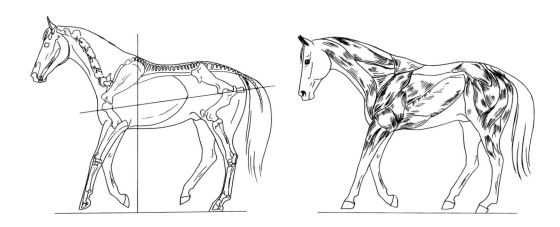

trying to push a rope up the street. The neck needs to have a certain amount of muscle so you have positive resistance against which to shape the energy that is coming up from the hindquarters. Where should the neck, the often overemphasized topline component be when the horse is moving? The answer is simple. If the hind end is working forward and the horse's back is relaxed and you are not pulling on the horse's mouth, his neck and head will find a natural position that is not only pleasing to look at but efficient as well.

Figure 20 and Figure 21. An unrestricted horse can move in a balanced fashion. (K.D. Blackwell)

The horse that is not restrained unreasonably up front will slightly flex the neck with each stride in response to the energy force sent from the hindquarters (Figures 20 and 21). The slight hinging of the neck in front of the withers, in effect, lightens the forehand. This slight curling also sends a small amount of energy back through the rider's hands and seat to the hindquarters. This further rounds the horse's back and allows it to be ready for the next driving stride.

If a horse has been trained to carry his head too low, his face behind the vertical (nose in), and the top of his neck very flat and still, his movement will lose its smoothness and efficiency at the expense of keeping a rigid head set (Figures 22 and 23). It would be like you carrying a stack of veterinary books around on top of your head as you did your chores. Your head and neck would become rigid and your body movements would be very stilted as you concentrated on keeping the books from falling. And you're not even loping! When a horse is forced to keep a rigid head set, he still must somehow dissipate the movement which is coming from the hind end. Since he has been trained not to flex or raise his neck at all, he instead lets his neck hinge downward (extend) which can create an overdeveloped underside to

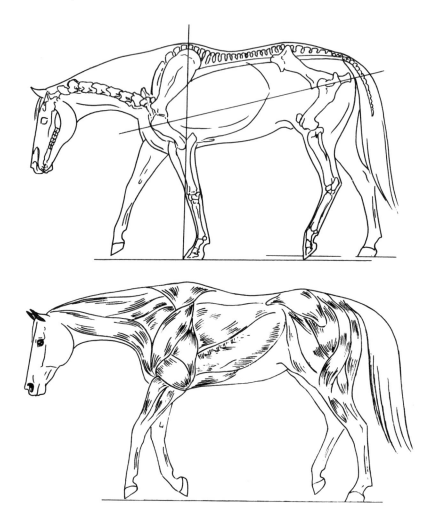

the neck and an underdeveloped topside. This upside down hinging breaks up the wave of energy around the horse's body. Rather than the energy being translated into a forward-reaching, efficient movement with a slightly upward rounding of the horse's body, much of the energy created by the hindquarters is broken up and lost.

Progression of Longitudinal Development aka Collection

The goal of developing a horse's body longitudinally is to be able to, at will, change the length and configuration of the horse's frame while at the same time maintaining the desired amount of forward energy and activity within the various frames. It is essential that a young horse (and all horses for that matter) is regularly and repeatedly encouraged to reach forward and fill up each frame in which they are worked. Great care must be taken to never cause a horse to look for a way to avoid heavy hands or he may overflex, get behind the bit, or refuse to move forward.

PHASES OF LONGITUDINAL DEVELOPMENT

The further along a horse is in his muscular development, fitness, and maturity, the easier it will be for him to perform increasingly difficult work. It takes a great deal of time and correct work to bring a horse to his optimum potential.

Phase A. Most young horses start out with one of two basic frames. The first is probably the most common. This horse carries itself with a shorter topline than underline (Figure 24). The horse holds his head high with his nose extended as much as 45 degrees in front of the vertical. His croup is higher than his withers and is held flat or up, causing the hind legs to trail behind the horse and the back to be hollow (photo 133). Gravity, the weight of the tack and rider, and a horse's intestinal fill all contribute to a hollow back. In addition, various conformational components will predispose a horse to have a hollow back and a horse

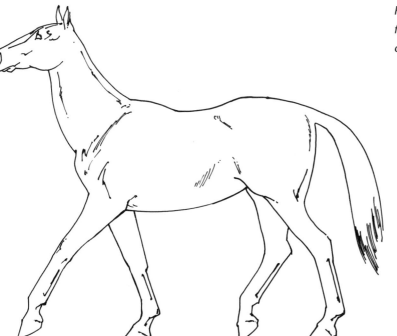

Figure 24. Starting frame—high-head carriage

133. During the first rides, a young horse often carries his nose 45 degrees or more in front of the vertical and has a croup higher than his forehand; in general, the horse is strung out.

with weak or poor muscle tone will display a hollow back, especially once his muscles have become tired.

The second type of beginning frame, sometimes seen in stock horses, is characterized by a horse that has a low, flat neck and a nose extended at about a 45-degree angle. Such a horse is often very heavy on the forehand and strung out behind but with a relatively flat, relaxed back. This horse has both a long topline and long underline (Figure 25).

Both types of beginning frames must be gradually developed so that they can strengthen and round their toplines, rock more weight back on the hindquarters, and increase the carrying capacity and activity of the

Figure 25. Starting frame—low-head carriage.

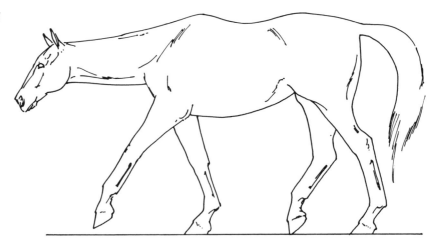

hind legs. A horse with the first type of beginning frame would benefit from long, low work such as posting trot.

The second type should be worked long and low only to accomplish suppleness and then he should be gradually introduced to the idea of shifting his weight rearward. Upward and downward transitions between halt, walk, and trot are a good means to initially cause the horse to step under with his hinds and slightly elevate his front end. This will take considerable time. It may take you several months or more to move from Phase A to Phase B. Phases C and D are phases too advanced for a young horse but are included for sake of completeness so that you know where you are headed. Do not be in a hurry. If you rush now, you will have to spend a lot of time later sorting out problems.

Phase B. After several months of riding, the young horse shows signs of slightly rounding the back accompanied by a very slight rounding of the neck and a slight lowering of the croup (photo 134, Figures 26 and 27). One of the most visible differences is that the horse can carry his nose comfortably and steadily at about 25 to 30 degrees in front of the vertical. The hind legs are stepping slightly more under the horse. It is beneficial to ride a young horse in this type of frame for the next phase of his training. He should show glimpses of self-carriage.

Of course, developing a horse's frame is a process accomplished by degrees. A horse should be ridden in a slightly more engaged frame for only a short period of time (a few strides, a few minutes) before he is allowed to return to his previous level of frame development or he is given a break on a long or loose rein.

134. The same horse a few months later showing more organization and balance to his movement because he is allowed a head carriage and nose position that is appropriate for a two-year-old in training.

*Figure 26. After
initial work—high-
headed horse.*

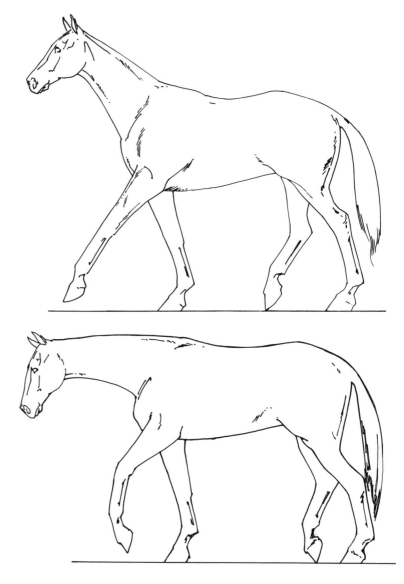

*Figure 27. After
initial work—low-
headed horse.*

Phase C. After a year or more under saddle, the young horse will show signs of moving into the next phase. Phase C is where a marked differentiation of frame will occur depending on the intended use of your horse. If destined for dressage, the horse should be encouraged to elevate the poll, drop the croup considerably and increase the flexion of the joints of the legs (Figure 28). Because such a configuration is not the goal for many types of western horses and hunters, the modified goal would be for a lower frame with the hindquarters not so engaged (Figure 29). However, in both cases, the horse should be allowed to carry his

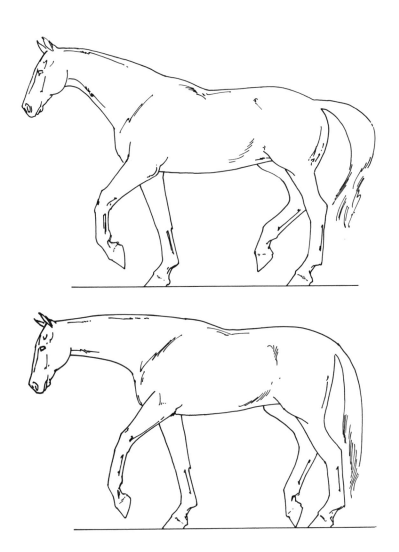

Figure 28. Beginning of self-carriage—dressage.

Figure 29. Beginning of self-carriage—western.

nose at about 10 to 15 degrees in front of the vertical. The horse should show self-carriage a great deal of the time by the time he has progressed to Phase C.

Phase D. In this final stage of high-level collection, the horse has an extremely shortened underline and rounded, stretched topline with an overall shortened frame from nose to tail. The poll should still be the highest point of the neck and the nose would be carried somewhere near the vertical or about 5 degrees in front of the vertical (Figure 30). The horse should be able to demonstrate self-carriage at almost any time when allowed to by the release of the inside rein or perhaps even both reins. This type of frame is appropriate for upper-level dressage horses

Figure 30. Collection.

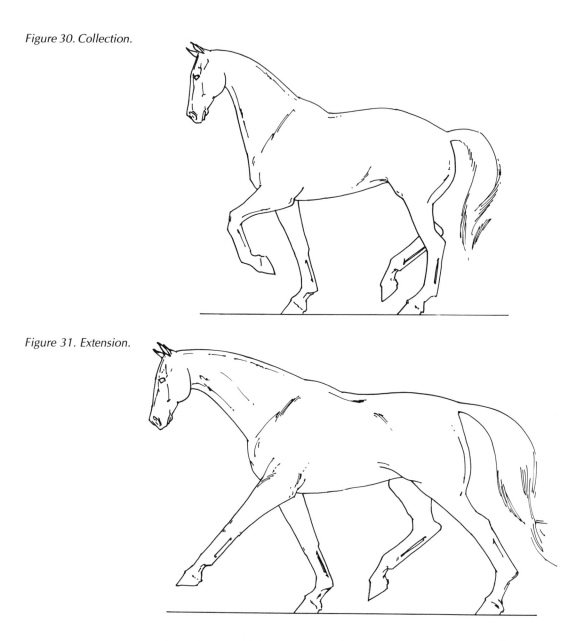

Figure 31. Extension.

and can be a goal for a senior reining or western equitation horse. Unfortunately, many horses, both English and western, have had "headset" configuration forced upon them in front but have not had the essential "engagement" collection developed behind, and therefore do not exhibit true, effective collection.

In order to maintain equilibrium, a collected horse assumes a posture or framework in accordance with the horizontal and vertical components of a maneuver, the speed of a maneuver, and the placement and movement of the rider. Extended maneuvers are characteristically more horizontal (Figure 31) while collected maneuvers are more vertical in nature (again refer to Figure 30). In spite of what it may seem, the horse's top line is actually the longest when it is in a collected frame due to the stretching of the longissimus dorsi. The gathered and compacted frame gives the illusion of a shortened topline.

During collection, the hindquarters are converted from a driving force to more of a supporting force, depending on the rider's regulatory aids. If a 1275-pound horse carries 175 pounds of rider and tack, he distributes the 1450-pound total weight differently for various maneuvers. Such a horse with a level topline and average balance and with virtually no influence exerted from the rider would, while standing, bear approximately 405 pounds on each foreleg and 320 or less with each hind leg. As the horse performs in a more collected frame, the hindquarters are required to bear an increasingly greater proportion of the load until, in the levade (a very balanced, controlled low rear) and during moments of the sliding stop, where all propulsion from the hindquarters has ceased, each hind leg bears 725 pounds. The horse collects by raising the head and neck above the body's mass, contracting the serratus ventralis which attaches the scapula to ribs, contracting the rhomboideus and trapezius, contracting the anterior pectorals, and flexing both hocks with the hind feet on the ground.

When lengthening of a movement is desired, remember that the goal is a greater distance covered per stride, not an increase in rate or tempo. Actually, in the transition to a lengthening, the tempo must be initially slowed to allow for the increased engagement of the hind limbs in order to result in a true increase in the length of stride. The limiting factor in stride length is the ability of the horse to flex the hip joint, which carries the femur and stifle and hock forward.

The extensor muscles of the hindquarters keep the horse in a state of appropriate engagement by preventing the hip joint from opening completely during extended movement. The more exaggerated the request, the more the horse moves with a springy and elastic forward swing of the hindquarters and back. Additionally, since the spinal column is lowered at the rear, the forehand is lightened and the muscles of the shoulder and forearm are able to experience freer and loftier.

PROBLEMS ENCOUNTERED WITH LONGITUDINAL DEVELOPMENT

If a rider's driving aids are too forceful or unbalanced to allow the horse to relax the longissimus dorsi, the horse may respond by hollowing his back and pushing out the abdominals in an attempt to escape the pain, or the horse may try to escape the back pain by holding his body in a crooked configuration. Since a horse's back is not really designed to carry a load anyway, hollowing and crookedness make the horse even more vulnerable to spinal problems. A hollow back is structurally weaker than an arched or flat back. The horse with a pot belly, or weak, bulging abdominals will have difficulty carrying itself in a collected frame for very many strides. The rider must effectively train and condition the horse to properly use the neck and abdominal muscles to relieve the back of some of its work. Gymnastics utilizing cavalletti lengthen, strengthen, and stretch the neck muscles; cantering and galloping condition the abdominals.

Conformation, poor saddle fit, and/or poor riding can cause a horse's back to be strained and he will hollow (dorsiflex or concave) it to avoid contact and pain. This results in a short topline and a long underline. The ligamentum nuchae and the supraspinous ligament slacken so there is no longer the necessary positive resistance for proper hind leg movement. The hind legs trail behind and the horse is heavy on the forehand (photo 135).

135. When a horse hollows his back he has a short topline and a long underline which causes his hind legs to trail behind and his head to be high.

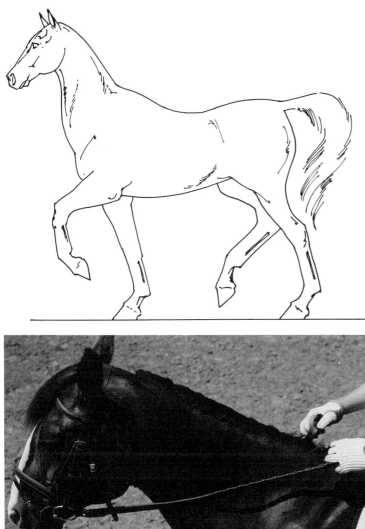

Figure 32. Above the bit with hollow back.

136. If a horse is not ridden to reach forward and downward for contact with the bit, he will not lengthen the topline of his neck (and back) but instead will let it fall slack allowing the under muscles of the neck develop (and bulge downward) as they support the weight of the head. (Compare with photo 16 on page 46.)

A horse that is forcibly held in a collected high "headset" will often bulge the muscles on the underside of the neck as a means of bracing against the rider's unyielding hand (see Figure 32). Also, if a horse is not encouraged to reach forward (from the hindquarters) for contact with the bit and to lengthen the top line of its neck, the under muscles of the neck (sternocephalicus, brachiocephalicus, sternohyoideus, and omohyoideus) can thicken (photo 136). Subsequently, the muscles on

137. In many cases it is the muscles just in front of the withers that need to be strengthened or the horse will develop a ewe neck.
(Compare the neck development in this "baby picture" to the same horse throughout Chapters 4-6.)

Figure 33. Behind the bit with hollow back.

the top of the neck receive inadequate development and can result in a flat or ewe neck with inadequate development of the neck muscles just in front of the withers (photo 137).

　　If a horse is ridden too strongly in the bridle, he may get behind the bit yet remain strung out behind. This also results in slack ligaments.

Without maximum tension on the ligaments, the horse cannot effectively use his neck or his back (Figure 33).

Lateral Development

As the horse develops longitudinally, he strengthens his entire body and will be better able to carry himself straight, that is, in lateral balance. A rider must be careful not to block a horse's action by improper riding. The shoulder can be blocked if there is a strong backward pull on a single rein which causes the base of the neck to be pushed off to the opposite side. See the discussion of lateral work in Chapters 5 and 6 for more information.

Select a horse that is well suited for the type of riding you enjoy. Then design his training and development program to help him reach his maximum performance potential. In that way, you will be making, not breaking the horse.

Supplemental Reading

Ainslie, Tom, and Ledbetter, Bonnie, *The Body Language of Horses,* Morrow, New York, 1980.

Crossley, Anthony, *Training the Young Horse,* Stanley Paul, London, 1978.

Dunning, Al, *Reining,* Western Horseman, Colorado Springs, CO, 1983.

Fiske, Jeanna C., *How Horses Learn,* Stephen Greene Press, Brattleboro, VT, 1979.

German National Equestrian Federation, *Advanced Techniques of Riding,* Half Halt Press, Gaithersburg, MD, 1986.

German National Equestrian Federation, *Principles of Riding,* Arco, New York, 1985.

Grant, Bruce, *How to Make Cowboy Horse Gear,* Cornell Maritime Press, Cambridge, MD, 1956.

Hill, Cherry, *Becoming An Effective Rider,* Garden Way, Pownal, VT, 1991.

Hill, Cherry, *From the Center of the Ring, An Inside View of Horse Competitions,* Garden Way, Pownal, VT, 1988.

Hill, Cherry, *Horsekeeping on a Small Acreage,* Garden Way, Pownal, VT, 1990.

Hill, Cherry, *The Formative Years, Raising and Training the Horse from Birth to Two Years,* Breakthrough, Ossining, NY, 1988.

Klimke, Reiner, *Basic Training of the Young Horse,* J. A. Allen, London, 1985.

Klimke, Reiner, *Cavalletti,* J. A. Allen, London, 1973.

Lewis, Lon D., *Feeding and Care of the Horse,* Lea & Febiger, Philadelphia, 1982.

Loomis, Bob, *Reining,* EquiaMedia Corp., Lomita, CA, 1991.

Miller, Robert W., *Western Horse Behavior and Training,* Doubleday Dolphin, New York, 1975.

Museler, Wilhelm, *Riding Logic,* Arco, New York, 1981.

Podhajsky, Alois, *My Horses, My Teachers,* Bright Books, Elverson, PA, 1987.

Podhajsky, Alois, *The Complete Training of the Horse and Rider,* Doubleday, Garden City, 1965.

Schusdziarra, H., M.D. and Schusdziarra, V., M.D., *An Anatomy of Riding,* Breakthrough, Ossining, NY, 1985.

Smythe, R. H., and Goody, P. C., *The Horse, Structure and Movement,* J. A. Allen, London, 1971.

Stashak, Ted (ed.), *Lameness in Horses,* 4th ed., Lea & Febiger, Philadelphia, 1987.

Waring, George H., *Horse Behavior,* Noyes, Park Ridge, NJ, 1983.

Glossary

action: the degree of flexion of leg joints during movement; also reflected in head, neck, and tail carriage.

age: as of January 1 of the year the horse was born.

aid: the means of communication with a horse.

    natural aids: mind, voice, seat (weight), legs, upper body, hands.

    artificial aids: crop, whip, spurs, running martingale.

agility: ability to change direction of the body or its parts rapidly.

agonist: a muscle (or group of muscles) which is the prime mover in an action, one which contributes to the desired movement by contraction.

antagonist: a muscle (or group of muscles), if contracted, which would cause a movement opposite to the desired movement of the agonist. Antagonists often provide a desirable resistance and stabilization to a movement.

attitude: a temporary behavior reflecting specific conditions.

back: a two-beat diagonal gait in reverse.

balance: ability to keep the center of gravity over the base to maintain equilibrium.

balk: to refuse or cease to move forward.

barn sour: herd-bound; bolting back to the barn.

bars (mouth): the bony, flesh covered space between the incisors and molars where the bit lies; interdental space. Part of the tree (saddle tree) that runs along each side and parallel to the horse's spine.

bell boots: protective boots that encircle the coronary band and bulbs of heels.

bend: the curve to the horse's body, most noticeable in the neck.

bending: lateral arcing of the body characteristic of circular work.

bight: a loop in a rope; end of the reins.

bit guard: a rubber or leather disc used with snaffle bit to prevent skin pinching.

bitting rig: a surcingle with rings through which driving lines may pass or to which side reins may be attached.

bosal: a rawhide noseband used as a bridle.

break-over: the moment in a horse's stride between landing and take off.

cadence: the rhythmic clarity of a gait.

canter: 3-beat gait; see lope.

cantle: the back of the seat of the saddle.

cavalletti: a type of ground rail.

cavesson: a leather noseband.

change of lead: change of the leading legs at the canter.

check: the western version of the half halt.

cinch: the band which fasten a western saddle in place.

cold-blooded: horses having ancestors that trace to heavy war horses and draft breeds. Characteristics might include more substance of bone, thick skin, heavy hair coat, shaggy fetlocks, and lower red blood cell and hemoglobin values.

collection: gathered together; a state of organized movement; a degree of equilibrium in which the horse's energized response to the aids is characterized by elevated head and neck, rounded back, "dropped croup," engaged hindquarters, and flexed abdominals. The horse remains on the bit, is light and mobile, and is ready to respond to the requests of the trainer.

colt: a young uncastrated male horse usually between the ages of weaning and gelding.

conditioned reflex: an acquired (learned) reaction.

conditioning: the process of developing tolerance to exercise and new capacities of performance.

connection: the relationship between the driving aids and the restraining aids and the response from the horse.

contact: the tightness of the reins related to the level of communication and flow of energy from rider's entire body to the horse and back again.

cooperative antagonism: the relationship between two muscle groups during a movement.

coordination: harmonious working of various muscles in a smooth, correct way with precise timing.

cue: signal or composite of trainer aids that is designed to elicit a certain reaction in a horse.

diagonal: pair of legs at the trot; the rider rises as the inside hind and outside front reach forward ("rise and fall with the leg on the wall").

disunited: cantering on different leads front and hind.

dressage: French for training or schooling; the systematic art of training a horse to perform prescribed movements in a balanced, supple, obedient, and willing manner.

dropped noseband: a noseband used with a snaffle bridle; designed to be below and over the bit which enhances sensitivity to the snaffle by stabilizing it on the bars.

engagement: the use of the horse's back and hindquarters to create energy and impulsion to forward movement. An engaged horse has a rounded topline, dropped croup, flexed abdominals and elevated head and neck.

equestrian: of or pertaining to horses or riding; a rider.

equestrienne: a female rider.

extension: a lowering and lengthening of a horse's frame and stride.

extinction: removal of a pleasant reinforcement to discourage the behavior it follows.

evasion: avoidance of an aid; for example, a horse that overflexes or gets "behind the bit" to keep from accepting contact with the bit.

fiador: a knotted throatlatch used in conjunction with a bosal, browband headstall, and horsehair reins. The knots of the fiador are the hackamore knot, the fiador knot and the sheet bend.

filly: a young female horse.

flexion: characteristic of a supple and collected horse. Vertical or longitudinal flexion, often mistakenly associated with "headset," is in reality an engagement of the entire body -- abdomen, hindquarters, back, neck and head.

flexibility: range of motion (contraction and extension) of muscles; lengthening and increased resiliency in tendons.

foal: a young male or female horse usually under a year old.

gelding: a castrated male horse.

gregarious: social, living in herds.

ground driving: the western version of long-reining.

habituation: repeated exposure to a stimulus thus decreasing the horse's response to it.

half halt: a calling to attention, a physical rebalancing of the horse, a prelude to transitions.

hot-blooded: horses having ancestors that trace to Thoroughbreds or Arabians. Characteristics might include fineness of bone, thin skin, fine hair coat, fine fetlock hairs, and higher red blood cell and hemoglobin values.

imprinting: the rapid learning in a young horse's first field of vision that reinforces species behavior.

impulsion: the desire, energy, and thrust from the horse's hindquarters characterized by a forward reaching rather than a backward pushing motion.

innate reflex: a reaction that is present intrinsically; inborn reaction.

instinct: inborn, intrinsic knowledge and behavior.

intelligence: ability to survive or adapt to man's world.

intermittent pressure: application and release of an aid in contrast to steady pressure.

jaquima: Spanish for hackamore; includes bosal, headstall, fiador, horsehair reins, and mecate.

jog: a slow Western trot.

kinesthetic sense: a sense of awareness (without using sight) of body position and action.

latent: assimilated learning that has not been demonstrated.

lateral: sideways movement; aids applied on a particular side of the horse.

lead: footfall pattern at the canter, inside legs reach farther forward than the outside legs: to the right, right hind leg and right foreleg reach farther forward than the left legs.

longitudinal flexion: a bowing upward of the horse's entire body which takes place in the vertical plane as opposed to lateral bending which takes place in the horizontal plane.

long rein: allowing a horse to stretch his neck toward the ground while still retaining light contact; in contrast to loose rein where there is no contact.

long yearling: a horse in the fall of its yearling year; usually eighteen months of age.

loose rein: allowing a horse to stretch to the ground without any contact on the rein—a totally slack rein.

lope: a three beat gait with an initiating hind leg, a diagonal pair including the leading hind leg and finally the leading foreleg.

mecate: a 22-foot horse hair rope, 3/8 to 3/4 inch diameter, that is fastened to a bosal to make reins and a lead.

modeling: observational learning or mimicry.

negative reinforcement: removing an unpleasant stimulus to encourage the behavior it follows.

nomadic: wandering or roaming

on the bit: a supple and quiet acceptance of contact with the bit.

panic snap: a snap with a quick-release collar; often used in horse trailers.

pecking order: caste system or social rank.

pivot: a crisp, prompt turn on the hindquarters.

poll: the junction of the vertebrae with the skull.

positive reinforcement: reward; giving something pleasant to encourage the behavior it follows.

power of association: the ability to link an action and a reaction; a stimulus and a response.

punishment: administering something unpleasant to discourage the behavior it follows.

range of motion: the amount of movement that can occur in a joint, expressed in degrees.

reflex: an immediate response to an stimulus situation

rein-back: back; a two-beat diagonal gait in reverse.

reinforcement: strengthening an association with primary or secondary reinforcers.

resistance: reluctance or refusal to yield or comply.

restraint: preventing from acting or advancing by psychological, mechanical, or chemical means.

rhythm: the sequenced placement of a horse's feet in a gait.

rounding: engagement characterized by an arched back, a dropped croup, hind legs well under the body, flexed abdominals and elevated head and neck.

serpentine: a series of half-circles and straight lines crossing from one side of the centerline to the other, requiring a change of direction each time the horse passes over the centerline.

shaping: the progressive development of the form of a movement; the reinforcement of successive approximations to a desired behavior.

shying: a horse stopping, jumping sideways, or bolting suddenly.

sidepass: moving the horse sideways, with no forward movement.

side reins: reins that are attached to a bitting rig or saddle while a horse is longed.

simple lead change: a change from one lead to another with a walk, trot, or halt in between.

skill: level of neuromuscular coordination.

snaffle: a bit that works on direct pressure with solid or jointed mouthpiece.

splint boots: protective covering worn around the cannon of the front legs to prevent injury.

straightness: that the horse's hind legs follow the front legs, relatively speaking.

strength: greatest force the muscles can produce in a single effort against resistance.

stride: the distance traveled in a particular gait, measured from the spot where one hoof hits the ground to where it next lands. Ten to twelve feet is the normal length of stride at a canter, for example.

substance: of solid quality as in dense bone or large body.

sullen: sulky, resentful, withdrawn.

supple: flexible.

surcingle: a piece of training tack that encircles the horse's heart girth and is used for longeing or driving.

temperament: the general consistency with which a horse behaves.

tendons: connective tissue which attaches muscle to bone.

terrets: rings on the surcingle (or harness) through which the reins pass.

transition: the upward or downward change between gaits and maneuvers; a change in speed or length of stride within a gait.

trot: a two-beat diagonal gait.

turn on the forehand: a maneuver in which the horse's hindquarters rotate around the forehand.

turn on the haunches (hindquarters): a maneuver in which the horse's forehand rotates around the horse' hindquarters.

vertical: in the vertical plane, that is, perpendicular to the horizon.

voice command: a natural training aid which must be consistent in word used, tone, volume, and inflection.

walk: a four-beat, flat-footed gait combining lateral and diagonal components: right hind, right front, left hind, left front.

yearling: a horse from January 1 to December 31 of the year following its birth.

Index